COUNT IT ALL JOY

A Faith Diary

JANET WILLIAMS-JOHNSON

COUNT IT ALL JOY

A Faith Diary

ISBN: 979-8-9881125-9-4

For information on the content of this book,
email: janetejoy1@att.net

JMPinckney Publishing Company, LLC
JMPinckneyPublishing@gmail.com

Printed in the United States of America

MEDITATE, THEN PRAY

There is a spiritual message depicted by James, a servant of God and the Lord Jesus Christ, to the twelve tribes, who were scattered abroad, when he declared in James 1:2 "My brethren, count it all joy when you fall into divers' temptations?" That question has stuck with me some 37 years as James' message in the text has served as a foundational message during my spiritual journey. "Count It All Joy" these four words assisted me through many spiritual trials designed by the Lord to test my faith, spiritual temptations of intentional enticements to disobey God's words, spiritual conflicts that often succumbed to two extremes, and spiritual heartbreaks that signified imbalances and blockages in my emotional well-being. Why would anyone want to count life's difficulties and classify them as joy? Yet, the phrase will not, has not, and cannot leave my thoughts.

Take a closer look at the four words in hopes of locating that spiritual message James addressed in the text:

Count, as a verb, is to determine the total number of a collection of items by units or groups. **It** is a pronoun referring to a thing previously mentioned.

All a predeterminer used to refer to the whole quantity or extent of a particular group.

Joy-a noun which is the state of being that allows one to experience feelings of intense long-last happiness and contentment of life.

TABLE OF CONTENT

INTRODUCTION

The world's definition for joy is "a feeling of great pleasure, happiness, and sharing tears of joy." The biblical definition of joy says that joy is "a feeling of good pleasure and happiness" that is dependent on who Jesus is rather than on who you are or what may be happening around you. In other words, "joy" is a learned behavior that rests in the Holy Spirit of God. What happens is you find yourself abiding in God's presence rather than the situations or circumstances of life.

Yet, the joy of the Lord has an in depth and greater meaning that is experienced over and over again on this level. As a little girl, I recall hearing my Grandmother Nellie saying; "this joy I have the world didn't give it to me, so the world can't take it away." She would be stirring around in the kitchen every morning preparing girts, eggs, and sausages for my siblings, cousins, and me. I heard her shouting about the joy of the Lord, time and time again. Yet, I didn't have a clue what she was sharing in those words.

As my life progressed and experiences came, it became so clear of my grandmother's message to me. Equally so, a tragic heart broke in life taught the full impact of that message. With my face dredged in tears, I heard while praying one morning: "Count It all Joy." My reply was; "who said that?" The hurt, emptiness, and despair in my heart did not, could not connect with the message I heard. My husband and father of my two children of thirteen years was killed in the bombing "Bierut, Lebanon. What is there to "count it all Joy" about right now! Who was trying to play a grueling trick with my mind? I heard the saying several more times. I know this quote was in the Bible, so I took a look at the scripture:

James 1:2 declares "My brethren, count it all joy when you fall into various trials. (NKJ) I read the verse over many times. Nothing grand happened right away, but over time, my sad countenance changed to a little glare of light shining through me. My husband's death wasn't the Joy, but how the Heavenly Father was going to keep me and my children in His perfect care was the Joy, I would come to know.

I began to jot down scriptures in a composition pad. Then I began to write poems to express my feelings of loneliness, despair, and how I was going to get through the difficult days ahead for my and my children's lives. After reading a morning devotional, sure enough, daily journaling eased my discontent.

Today, my daily declaration is: "Count It All Joy!"

PREFACE

My prayer journals date back to September 1992. Wow! Always I had the desire to share my thoughts in those journals with others, but life experiences always seemed to get in the way of writing this collection of journal prayers.

The death of my dear mother on March 10, 2020, and my beloved sister on March 27, 2021, brought so much sadness into my life. How was I ever going to rebound from this deep grief? Then, my health began to create concerns as both of my knees were riddled with osteoarthritis causing severe pain in both knees. Joint knee replacement was needed in both knees. So, I went through physical therapy to prepare me for knee replacement surgery in August 2021. The day before my scheduled surgery, I learned that my surgery was postponed because COVID 19 patients were flooding the hospital limiting inpatient admission. I was devastated and the pain in my knees were now causing my hips and back to surrender with insurmountable pain.

Yet, the presence of the Lord was with me. In my prayer and meditation time, the song: "I've learned how to live holy, I've learned how to learn right, I've learned how to suffer, for if I suffer, I'll gain eternal life." I said," I need relieve now." I heard; "eternal life" does not always mean death. Rejoice in eternal life, that is right now in the spiritual realm as I am setting everything right. Just trust me!" My writing process began anew.

I decided to write a foundational prayer journal to symbolize the foundational number "twelve." Count it all joy.

This Faith Diary has a collection of 78 prayers that symbolizes a synonym for joy. My prayer is that this devotional brings joy, happiness and gladness to your life.

Yours in Christ,
Janet Williams-Johnson

Bundle of Joy

ONE-SYMBOLIZE OF UNITY IN JUBILATION

To show **Jubilation** in unity is a **feeling of extreme joy** that marks happy events, and the utterance of expressing sounds forming a complete and pleasing wholeness. When you "Count It All Joy" with unity in jubilation, whatever is against you must die, in the name of Christ Jesus.

1. THE VOICE

Jeremiah 33:11 - The voice of jubilation, and the voice of joy, the voice of the bridegroom, and the voice of the bride, the voices of those who say, "Praise Yahweh of hosts, for Yahweh is good, for his loyal love is forever," the voices of those who bring thank offerings to the house of Yahweh, for I will restore the fortunes of the land as in the beginning,' says Yahweh.

Gracious God, Our Father, humbly we bow to claim this day's promises of Jubilation in You. Your promises give strength to complete every task You ordained for my hands today. Your promises establish power to speak those things that are not into existence by the power of Your Holy Spirit that dwells within me. Your promises provide authority to walk by faith and not by sight because I am the called-out conquer to proclaim Your kingdom agenda. Your promise brings confidence in You Heavenly Father that You are God and You change not leading me through the curtain of heaven into Your inner sanctuary.

I stand on your oath which is all truth and cannot lie, as You are truth, secure in Your will and Ways. Thank You for your promises and oath that remain in unconditional openness, honesty, and sincerity keeping me from sins, transgression and iniquities. Your truth and promises of Jubilation, Heavenly Father, gives me encouragement, assurance, and peace.

Thank You Lord, for hearing and answering this prayer!

TWO-SYMBOLISM OF DIVISION IN EXULTATION

Exultation through division occurs **through a feeling of great happiness and excitement releasing a refreshed spirit of worship singing songs to glorify God** and canceling out separation through renewed discernment. When you "Count It All Joy" with division in exultation, you can leap for joy declaring you are the winner in Christ Jesus.

1. POSITION ME

Psalm 46:10 - Be still, and know that I am God! I will be honored by every nation. I will be honored throughout the world."

Heavenly Father, I come now thanking You for this morning. It is a new day filled with Your glory, honor, and praise extending new mercies to me. I am grateful for Your Word declaring, I am the salt of the earth; "world seasoning" to affect my surroundings with love, joy, peace, perseverance, long-suffering, meekness, gentleness, and self-control (Galatian 5:22-23). Don't allow me to be worthless or void of Your flavor. I want to bring out positive seasoned behaviors to Your people.

Position me to speak-up against those things that are not pleasing in your sight and wound the Body of Christ. Psalm 37: 28 declares; "For the Lord loves justice and He will never abandon the godly." Grant me now godly wisdom to stand as Your light of justice to those actions, deeds, mannerism and thoughts that will not, cannot line-up with Your will and ways.

Let the light of You, shine on me, Abba Father. "Shine on me! Let the light from Your lighthouse shine one me." Help me, to be a shining center of light, lifting up all people in the name of Jesus Christ.

Thank You, Lord for hearing and answering this prayer.
Amen

2. IN THE SEARCH

Psalm 63:1 - O God, you are my God; I earnestly search for you. My soul thirsts for you; my whole-body longs for you in this parched and weary land where there is no water.

Gracious God, the Creator of Heaven and Earth, I am excited this morning to declare that You God never grows faint or weary to hear Your children call on You. Never will I compare You to anyone for there is no image resembling not equal to You the Holy One.

You created the stars and morning by morning, You call each by its name. Counting them to be certain that none are lost or strayed away.

With clarity of thoughts, I am well able to know that You see all my troubles and hear my pending cases. When I feel all of life crushing, causing me to not go another step. Surely, I recall that You never grow faint or weary, never too tired or too busy to assist and listen to my cry for help.

So, humbly, I wait on You, Lord with renewed strength. I am free to fly high on wings like eagles. I am well able to run and not grow weary. I am capable to walk and not faint. Yes, I know that the Lord is the everlasting God, the Creator of all the heavens and earth.

Thank You Lord, for hearing and answering this prayer!

THREE-SYMBOLISM OF TRINITY IN TRIUMPH

To triumph in the trinity is the act, fact, or condition of being victorious in a conquest with significant success or noteworthy achievement. Then allow yourself to know that God exists as three persons, the Father, Son, and Holy Spirit; as these three are one so that there is one God. When you "Count It all Joy" with triumph in the trinity and pray the manifestation of God, is one in essence and three in person.

1. ASSURANCE

Deuteronomy 20:4 - For the LORD your God is the one who goes with you to fight for you against your enemies to give you victory."

God, my Father, the author and finisher of my faith. I come now to bless and adore You and the divine refuge for my life. I do not take this opportunity lightly to call on Your Holy and awesome name.

I release my heart and mind to pray seeking your forgiveness for my sins, transgressions and iniquities in this new day. Take the lead in my life to a plain path. Wash me clean from my guilt. Purify me from my negative ways.

With a heart of thanksgiving, I devote myself to pray and stand in a fervent position of persistent prayer, now. With Your divine help, I can remain standfast, unmovable, and watchful praying only expression of faith in You, Abba Father.

Today, I stretch out in confident assurance that what I hope for is going to happen as the evidence of things I cannot yet see are manifested. (Hebrews 11:1) I believe and stand in flat-footedness that the promises of God to me will do what it says according to God's will, purpose, and plan for my life. Lord, I thank You that my faith will not die, as I am encouraged to pray and wait on the Lord in great expectations.

Thank You Lord, for hearing and answering this prayer!

2. CHRIST'S MIND

Colossian 2:15 - He disarmed the rulers and authorities[a] and put them to open shame, by triumphing over them in him.

Heavenly Father, it amazes me that You know my name and reserved grace for me in Christ Jesus even before time began. No words of man or spirit matters except the words You speak concerning me. I approach Your throne of grace not with my small level of intellect or speaking ability, but I come in Your Knowledge, Lord. Holy Spirit help and guide me into all truth.

Even in the joy of Your love, I am unable to see, to hear, and imagine the beauty of those things You, God, has prepared for me and everyone that loves You.

Lord, I thank You that the mind of Christ is available to me by the Holy Spirit. So, I take a deep breath to concentrate on God's wonderful plan of salvation through Christ Jesus.

Thank You, Holy Spirit through You I can begin to know "the mind of Christ."

Thank You Lord, for hearing and answering this prayer!

3. THIS AND THAT

Proverbs 28:13 - When the righteous triumph, there is great glory, but when the wicked rise, people hide themselves.

Because You are my rock in ages past and a shelter from the stormy path, I pause to bless Your majestic name, Heavenly Father. I testify that: You are a bridge over troubled waters. You are a light unto my path in dark and slippery places. You are a wheel in the middle of a wheel propelling me forward in You.

When the enemy came in like a flood, I testify that you upheld a mighty standard that brought me through the "this and that" of life's situations. When the wind of confusion blew into my family, I testified that you positioned me to stand firm from the wiles of the enemy. When disappointments come, turning my world upside down, I testify that You remain a faithful friend.

Sweet Jesus for being that pure white handkerchief that dried my tears, calmed by fear, and told me to run on to see what the end will be. I testify that You covered me with Your saving grace.

Thank You Lord, for hearing and answering this prayer!

FOUR-SYMBOLISM OF PERFECTION IN REJOICE -

Perfection in rejoice is how you learn to demonstrate the fruit of the Spirit: love, joy, peace, perseverance, kindness, goodness, faithfulness, gentleness, and self-control. When you "Count It All Joy, it provides inner gladness which leads to a cheerful heart and behavior.

1. SEE THE HARVEST

John 4:35 - [35] Do you not say, 'It is still four months until the harvest comes?' Look, I say to you, raise your eyes and look at the fields *and* see, they are white for harvest.

Our Father and our God, in adoration I bow to magnify and honor Your holy name. You are an ever-present refuge, strong tower, and a maker way. I praise You for who You are. You are good and know how to give good gifts to Your children.

Your strength, power, and might, give me everything I need to wait for the harvest to manifest in my life and the lives of my family members. While we wait forgive me of any words, thoughts, deeds, or actions that I committed that wounded Your kingdom plan, purpose and will for me.

Take complete authority over this day directing every element to cooperate with Your divine purpose and destiny for me and my family. I know the fields are white and ready for the harvest. But I need You to ready for this work in You.

Saturate my mind for this season of success and prosperity according to Your will. Download good health, vision, direction, ingenuity, creativity, spirituality, holiness, righteousness, peace, and resourcefulness from Your endless supply of gifts in my life for Your glory.

Give me a fresh excitement to worship You. Restore a fresh mindset to think clearly and positively in You. Establish a fresh zeal to serve You with a clean and pure heart. Rub a fresh anointing that is uncontaminated and unpromised by cluttered destruction and desire of my flesh.

While I wait for You Heavenly Father, let Your will be done in my life.

2. AN APPROVED WORKER

2 Timothy 2:15-17 - Do your best to present yourself to God as one approved, a worker who does not need to be ashamed and who correctly handles the word of truth. [16] Avoid godless chatter, because those who indulge in it will become more and more ungodly. [17] Their teaching will spread like gangrene. Among them are Hymenaeus and Philetus.

Heavenly Father, help me to ready my mind, heart and spirit to take the next step in You will, plan and purpose for my life. Detox my soul of the poison accumulated by unhealthy actions and exploits that caused me not to live my authentic life in You.

I want to be that approved and dependable worker in Your vineyard. Never ashamed to rightly divide and handle Your Word in all I do and speak.

Season my tongue with words of godly wisdom to avoid gossip, malicious, and hurtful declarations that cause deep penetrating wounds to my brothers and sisters. Purge me with Hyssop, morning, noon, and night to dwell always in Your compassion, love and support for the Body of Christ.

Teach me Heavenly Father to spread the good News of Jesus' salvation everywhere I go. My aim, desire, and agenda is to serve You in spirit and truth. While I am on this journey, keep me in peace, love, joy, hope, and grace in You.

Direct and guide me to concentrate on doing
my best for You, Heavenly Father.
Amen!

3. REJOICE IN THE LORD

Deuteronomy 12:7 - There also you and your households shall eat before the Lord your God, and rejoice in all your undertakings in which the Lord your God has blessed you.

My Father, who art in heaven, Holy is Your name. I come now to release the weight of all burdens-regrets-disappointment= challenges on You, Lord. You are my sustainer, the lifter of my concerns. Your word declared that You will never allow the consistently righteous to be moved from Your presence, made to slip, fall or fail in the mighty name of Jesus

Because you have rendered me weightless when I place my trust in You, I have everything good action, deed, and thought to maintain the right attitude of thankfulness and gratitude to You, Abba Father.

Your plans, purpose and position for my life allow me weightlessly to see through spiritual eyes and guide me into all truth. Lord keep me in Your desired guidance that displays less of me and more of You to greater glory.

Listen ever so lovingly to my cry for greater love, grace and mercy on this day. Listen to my voice in the morning, at noon, and into the evening, oh Lord. My God.

Thank You Lord, for hearing and answering this prayer!

4. SING FOR JOY!

Psalm 5:11 - But let all who take refuge in You be glad, let them ever sing for joy;

Our Father, who art in heaven, I come now to honor and praise You. Asking that You reveal who You are to me this day. Set this world right for Your glory: for You know what's best for Your children. Because I know You to be a good and awesome God, I yield my will to You and say thank You: for Your forgiveness allowing me to know how easy it is to forgive others that trespass against me.

I say yes Lord to Your way, Your will, Your divinely changing all things for my good. I want to make the connection between what God does and what I do today. Guide and direct me to reflect back reminding myself that it was You God, that brought me through some many disappointments, heartbreaks, misunderstandings, and negative thoughts.

Thank You Lord, for hearing and answering this prayer!

In You, I know how to sing for joy, so I reinforce that:

- That my kingdom name is released and all that You ordained and assigned to me are picking me up in the realm of the spirit.
- That I am forgiven of all my sins and become a new creature in Christ Jesus.
- That I am divinely seated in heavenly place in Christ Jesus and a part of the royal priesthood.
- That I am accepted in the Beloved and free from condemnation.
- That I am sealed with the Holy Spirit of promise in Christ Jesus.

Jump for Joy

FIVE- SYMBOLISM OF GRACE IN ELATION

Grace in elation can be classified as **divine influence operating in your life**. There is unmerited favor, regeneration, and sanctification with virtuous impulses as a spontaneous gift from God almighty. Great happiness and exhilaration may even fill you with joy. When you "Count It All Joy in grace in elation, you are marked by high spirits and heightened joy with exaggerated optimism.

1. SHELTER WITH GOD

Psalm 11:1 - In the LORD I take refuge. How then can you say to me: "Flee like a bird to your mountain.

Abba Father, the All-Seeing and Knowing One, that art in heaven. May Your name be honored as we humbly bow in Your presence. May Your Kingdom come; may Your Will be done on earth just as it is in heaven. Give us our natural and spiritual food for today, and forgive us, don't look on our sins, transgressions, and iniquities, just as You instructed us to forgive those who sinned against us. Help us, keep us, and allow us to yield not into temptation but deliver us consistently from the evil one!

I pause to take refuge in You, Jehovah Jireh, the great provider, who sees my future as well as my present. You are well able to supply my needs. I calm myself to take protection in You Jehovah Nissi, my banner, who is powerful enough to overcome my foes in lands near and far. Speak to the hearts and minds of disobedient men and women to humble themselves to Your authority. Keep me in Your grace to trust, call, and ask that You lift-up a divine standard in the lives of Your people today.

Gladly, I am that You are watching closely to examine every thought, deed, intention, action, and secret meeting that does not bring glory to your kingdom on earth. In Your renewed grace and excitement, I delight in Your righteousness. No looking back, no turning back, all the way in You Abba Father.

Thank You, Lord, for hearing and answering this prayer.

2. HIGHWAY OF HOPE

Isaiah 35:8 - And a highway will be there; it will be called the Way of Holiness; it will be for those who walk on that Way. The unclean will not journey on it; wicked fools will not go about on it.

Holy Spirit of God, I bow to worship, glorify and honor Your presence. You are alpha and omega; the beginning and the end. I worship You as the source of infinite hope and grace. I rest Jehovah Shalom, the Lord my peace. What a joy divine to know that You are loaded with wholeness, completeness, wellness, and safety.

I confess my sins, those immoral acts that led to transgressions and iniquities. Hide my grossly unfair behaviors in the shadow of Your wings.

I thank You, God, for the glorious promises in Your eternal Word. You are lighting a flame of hope in my heart every second, minute, and hour of this new day.

Hold at bay the furious storms of life that are raging with devastating winds today. Sustain my aim, desire, and hope to remain on the devotion highway of faith in You, Heavenly Father.

You are an anchor of hope for Your children. When the enemy comes making in like a flood, I rely on Your Holy standard to lift me up in You. Surely, I can tell the storms of life to obey the Master of the sea.

You are my comfort of hope for my children, family, and friends. Continue to guide, guard, and direct them from despair. Establish their surefootedness with strength making their ways perfect with lasting hope of You.

Allow hopefulness to become a daily habit to achieve a permanent joyful spirit in You. Keep me steadfast, unmovable as I travel on the road, the highway of hope.

Thank You, Lord, this is the way to holiness.

3. HOPE IN GOD

Jeremiah 1:4-5 - The word of the LORD came to me, saying, "Before I formed you in the womb I knew[a] you, before you were born I set you apart; I appointed you as a prophet to the nations."

Elohim, the creator of heaven and earth, who separated light from darkness, water from dry land, and night from day I pause to bless Your creative authority, power, and sovereignty. Great is thy faithfulness, oh Lord, my Father, morning by morning new immeasurable mercies I see. I am so glad to "hope in You, God.

I confess my sins, transgressions, and iniquities seeking repentance now that are too numerous to name. I seek repentance, forgiveness that David declared in Psalm 51. Purify me from my sins and I will be clean. Wash me from my impurities and make me whiter than snow. How glad I am to have Your renewed joy, a clean heart, and the right spirit returned unto me. Again, I am lifted up to "hope in You, God.

With my mouth filled with gladness, gentleness, love, meekness, peace, praise, and self-control, I thank You. I hope exciting in Your presence God. Singing new songs of praise that allow grace to abound during the night as we slumber and sleep. Happy I am to hope in You, God.

I hope in Your healing over sicknesses and diseases. I hope in Your grace that is always available to me. I hope in Your protection, when the enemy comes in like a flood Your righteous, holy, unsinkable standard is lifted-up. I hope in Your blood covering that hides me from the scourge of the enemy. Abba Father, I hope in Your love.

4. HOPE IN THE LIGHT

Isaiah 60:19 - The sun will no more be your light by day, nor will the brightness of the moon shine on you, for the LORD will be your everlasting light, and your God will be your glory.

Jehovah Nissi, the God who is powerful enough to overcome any foe. I lifted up my hands to the throne of You, oh God, believing, depending, and trusting that You will be at war against my enemies. Because there is no greater power in heaven or earth, I ask Jehovah Nissi that You increase hope lights in my life today.

All that I am and all I hope to become, I press toward the mark of Your high calling that is in Christ Jesus. I greet today with great anticipation of your goodness and mercy. Prepare for today's tasks.

Restore a fresh excitement and zeal in my mind to increase a new anointing in You. I declare that I am saved in Your hope of lights.

Thank You, Lord, that hope in the light will cause me to trust You enough to ask for the impossible in Your strength to knowledge and understand how able You are to fulfill your promises in all things.

Keep my cup filled so that I may lift it up to You always. Continue to quench that thirst inside me. Bread of hope and heaven feed me. Equip me, establish me, and reign with me until I want no more. Just keep my cup of hope filled in Your impossibilities until I want and desire no more.

5. HOPE IN STRENGTH

Jeremiah 16:19 - LORD, my strength and my fortress, my refuge in time of distress, to you the nations will come from the ends of the earth and say, "Our ancestors possessed nothing but false gods, worthless idols that did them no good.

Almighty everlasting God, the creator of heaven and earth, I bow to worship and dwell in Your presence. You are Jehovah Tsuri, the Lord my rock. He, who stands in permanence, protection, and enduring faithfulness.

I hope in Your strength to confess my sins, transgressions, and iniquities that continue to hinder my spiritual growth in You. Renew my mind, heart, and soul to the righteousness of you Oh, God.

Then grant me the opportunity to praise and glorify Your worthy name. You are always available to hear my humble call unto You. Strengthen me in my wait for You. Do not allow Your promises to pass me by, oh Lord. I don't always understand why my trials are so many. Yet, I trust and depend on You to bring me through with joy unspeakable.

Develop my character to know who I am in You. Teach me to speak that God's anointing destroys every yoke in my life. I want to know completely how to function in Your divine order according to Your divine systems of protocol. Keep reminding me each day that I am getting warmer and not colder in my search to know and experience Your godly strength day by day.

In Jesus name, I bless Your holy name, Abba Father.
Amen!

SIX-SYMBOLISM OF TESTING IN BLISS

Testing in bliss may be **finding out how well something works**. You take a closer look at the quality, performance and reliability. It may lead you to ask, what level of knowledge or skill did I acquire. You may even find yourself in perfect happiness and great joy. When you "Count It All Joy" while testing in bliss, utter joy and contentment may feel like you have a perfect life, joyfulness and whole.

1. GOD'S PROMISE BRINGS HOPE

Hebrews 6:18 - He has given us both his promise and his oath, two things we can completely count on, for it is impossible for God to tell a lie. Now all those who flee to him to save them can take new courage when they hear such assurances from God; now they can know without doubt that he will give them the salvation he has promised them.

Abba Father, the all-knowing, the all-righteous, and holy one that resides in heaven. Hallowed be Your majestic, excellent, extraordinary name. Lord, let Your kingdom come with promises that bring hope today.

I confess that I have moved the measure from your divine mark on yesterday and previous days. I need You to set me right to receive your promises of hope. So, set me right with You, now in the name of Christ Jesus. Wash me again so that I am whiter than snow. Allow me now to hear Your joy and gladness. I want to be satisfied in your hope this day.

Please hide Your face from my sins and blot out all my guilt and stains. Prepare and make me eager to face today's challenges because I know that You, Lord, are with me.

In Your hope, I expect positive outcomes, sufficient grace, loving-kindness, and tender mercies.

Thank You, lord for providing everything
I need to face this day in You. Amen.

2. BE NOT ASHAMED

Romans 1:15-16 - [15] That is why I am so eager to preach the gospel also to you who are in Rome. [16] For I am not ashamed of the gospel, because it is the power of God that brings salvation to everyone who believes: first to the Jew, then to the Gentile.

Tribune God that sits high and looks low, let me dwell in Your presence. How hallowed, holy, righteous, perfect, marvelous, and majestic is Your name. Strengthen me now to stand firmly in Your will being done on earth as it is in heaven.

Humbly, I seek today's daily bread of forgiveness of my sins, transgression, and iniquities in all my unstable ways. Release me now of resentments, misunderstandings, heartaches, disappointments, jealousy, backbiting so that I am well able to stand firmly in the gospel of Jesus Christ.

You have shown me and allowed me to know because of grace and mercy, morning by morning there is the power of God in salvation for everyone who believes. This day, I proclaim and shout loudly great is thy faithfulness. Also immeasurable is your compassion that withstands and fails not.

This today, tomorrow and forever, I will not be ashamed of the gospel, its authority and power decreed and declared to me. I pause, take a deep breath in this clear conscience moment asking You Abba Father to heal the land. Then, my eyes to be opened and attentive to offer prayers in this sanctified place.

3. RENEWED ZEAL

Galatians 5:7-10 - You were running a good race. Who cut in on you to keep you from obeying the truth? [8] That kind of persuasion does not come from the one who calls you. [9] "A little yeast works through the whole batch of dough." [10] I am confident in the Lord that you will take no other view. The one who is throwing you into confusion, whoever that may be, will have to pay the penalty.

With renewed zeal and excitement, humbly Heavenly Father, I bow to adore, Your divinely great presence. You are Jehovah Jireh, that great provider, who sees our future as well as our past and present. You are well able to supply my needs.

With renewed zeal and fervor, humbly Heavenly Father, I bow to worship you as Jehovah Nissi, my banner. Who is powerful enough to overcome my foes near and far. With renewed zeal and love, humbly Heavenly father, I bow to glorify You as Jehovah Tsidkenu, the Lord my righteousness because You intervened on my behalf to restore me to Your likeness and fellowship with You.

With renewed zeal and avidity, humbly Heavenly Father, I bow to exalt You as Jehovah Roi.

I flow in my renewed zeal to pull down strongholds, cast down vain imagination and every negative thought, action, word, or deed that lifts itself against the knowledge of Christ Jesus as Lord and Savior of this world.

Flow Holy Spirit, with a fresh zeal that will release me from every yoke of brokenness in my life and the lives of my children, grandchildren, family and friends. Keep me covered in Your prayer shield anointing, fire wall, and smoke screens today.

4. BE STILL

Luke 4:18-19 - The Spirit of the Lord is on me, because he has anointed me to proclaim good news to the poor. He has sent me to proclaim freedom for the prisoners and recovery of sight for the blind, to set the oppressed free, [19] to proclaim the year of the Lord's favor."

Abba Father, the holy and righteous God, who created and sustains all things. humble, I bow to worship You. Yes, You are all-powerful, all-knowing, ever-present help, who loves me, Your child with a never-ending love.

Let Your will be done, here on earth as it is in heaven. Give me my nourishment and spiritual wisdom for this day. Forgive me my sins, transgression, and iniquities just as I forgive this one or that one who sinned, transgressed against me. Keep me steadfast, unmovable so that I do not yield to temptations in my actions, words, or deeds, but assist me to remain delivered from the evil one. I declare that I will "be still" and wait on You, Abba Father.

Every element of this day I bow now and will cooperate with Your destiny, divine, plan, and purpose for my life, the lives of my children, grandchildren, family and friends in the name of Christ Jesus. Keep my loved ones safe from disobedient ideas that may what to lift-up its ugly head.

I say, "Thank You Abba Father" that seasons of frustrations and failure are rendered null and void now, because the name of Christ

Jesus gave a halt and placed a moratorium on the enemy's destructive moments and negative activities. Jehovah Nissi, keep high and lift up a standard and banner of truth, letting all creations hear Your clarion call to trust, travail, and wait on You, Abba Father.

> *Oh Lord, I cry-out, save all of creation from themselves.*
> *Give everything needed to "be still" in You Abba Father.*

5. JOY

Nehemiah 8:9-10 -Then Nehemiah the governor, Ezra the priest and teacher of the Law, and the Levites who were instructing the people said to them all, "This day is holy to the LORD your God. Do not mourn or weep." For all the people had been weeping as they listened to the words of the Law.[10] Nehemiah said, "Go and enjoy choice food and sweet drinks, and send some to those who have nothing prepared. This day is holy to our Lord. Do not grieve, for the joy of the LORD is your strength."

Heavenly Father, with weeping eyes and on bended knees, I humble myself in your present. I honor You as my refuge, deliver, strong tower, and an awesome way-maker. Restore unto me, Your joy that this world can never give nor can take away in You.

In renewed joy, I release my mind of proud and naughty thoughts, letting go of arrogant behaviors, and offer my body, spirit, and soul in a spirit of total submission to You. Forgive me, I deeply apologize for those times I thought too much of myself. Your renewed as saved me and set every captive intention free.

Right now, I am excited to have Your fill of joy as a time to celebrate Your good gifts today: life, health, strength, peace, love, and self-control. I am strengthened spiritually and filled with Your joy divine.

In a spirit of gladness, I bow to put Your joy into the atmosphere that is filled with Your promises and goodness. I declare and decree that Your joy is an inner quality that always is available to me, my children, grandchildren, spouse, parents, siblings, family and friends in the name of Christ Jesus.

Your joy is a part of my very nature to overcome feelings of loss to abundance, sadness to cheerfulness, and depression to elation in the blessed name of Christ Jesus.

Thank You, Lord, that Your joy brings beauty that
touches my heart.

6. MY LIFE TESTIMONY

Psalm 71:4 - My God, rescue me from the power of the wicked, from the clutches of cruel oppressors.

Our Father, the Sovereign God of the universe. I stand still to give my life's testimony in glory, honor, and praise of who You are in this new day. It is great to call You my light and salvation. I have no need to fear because You are always available to me.

Keep on forgiving my debts as I made the decision to forgive him or her that trespassed against me. I am grateful that You hold me tightly, never allowing me to fall into temptation and blocking the evil one from my life.

With my hands lifted-up and my heart filled to the brim with praise, I thank You once again for Your unfailing love and compassion filled with promises. Hear my cries and don't keep looking at my sins, transgressions, and iniquities. Remove the stain of guilt and create in me clean hearts, O God, and renew a right spirit within me. Don't banish me from Your presence and take Your Holy Spirit from me.

I feel Your divine protection, deep peace, and security always with me. Lord, I thank You. I pray that Your power reign with me every second, minute, and hour this day. Don't forget to fill me with renewed hope, freedom, and an incredible reason to live in Your Kingdom, Heavenly Father. I desire to walk in an attitude of gratitude flowing abundantly in Your favor to speak how God's anointing destroys every yoke in and around my life.

SEVEN-SYMBOLISM OF COMPLETION IN GRATIFICATION

Completion in gratification is **an action of finishing something as a forward pass on life's journey. It might be gained from the satisfaction of a desire in the promises of God.** When you "Count It All Joy" with completion in gratification, you experience a pleasurable emotional reaction of happiness to fulfillment of a desired goal.

1. DELIVERANCE
Psalm 9:1-10

All my heart will give thanks to You, Eternal One. I will tell others about Your amazing works.

Gracious almighty God, our Father, the all-sufficient, all-knowing, and all-seeing God of the universe. Humbly, I pause to honor, magnify, and glorify Your marvelous majestic, precious, and wonderful name. you are Holy, righteous, the protect God El Elyon, our only Judge.

Because Your set-time of deliverance and favor are in Your hand, I acknowledge that You are The God of heaven and earth. Hallowed are You will and ways in all areas of my life.

With divine deliverance, I stand intentional to proclaim prayer as a sacred communication and way of feelings connected to You, God as well as to my brothers and sisters in You heavenly Father.

I lift my voice in adulation to honor You God as my strength, rock of ages, steadfast love, my fortress, and a dependable shield. I am so thankful that prayer unto You brings renewed awareness of Your divine identity.

In Your deliverance, every second, minute, and hour of this day, I stand in affirmative prayers to sustain this heartbreaking, disappointments, misunderstanding challenges on life's journey with confidence. Amen!

2. GRACE

Hebrews 4:16

[16] So let us come boldly to the throne of our gracious God. There we will receive his mercy, and we will find grace to help us when we need it most.

Because Your grace is built on nothing else than Jesus' blood and righteousness, I bow on bended knees to worship You, the Great I Am, Heavenly Father. In Your presence I ask that You reveal Your magnificent unchanging and wholeness of grace to me on this day. You do what is best for me just as You do with excellence in the heavens above me and in earth.

Deliver, keep, and restore me alive, safe, and healthy with daily nutritional meals. Enlarge my heart to forgive others just as You constantly forgive my trespasses and debts. Keep me safe from my personal thoughts, deeds, and actions. You are in charge of heaven and earth and will be able to do all things You want anytime and any day.

In Your divine grace, I stand in prayer with Your plans and purposes for this day. Thank You, heavenly Father for Your dear Son, Christ Jesus that took on the shame of the cross for me and allowed men to humiliate Him.

I can't help but think of Your goodness and all You have done for me. This grateful soul cries loudly, hallelujah, thank You Lord for healing and saving me from false burdens, liars, character assassins, gossipers, loneliness, heaviness, oppressions, and depressions.

In mediation and prayer, You taught me how to cast everything upon You in faith. Yes, Lord, Your grace is sufficient for me.

3. THE WEIGHT OF YOUR PROBLEM

Psalm 55:16 - But I will call on God and the LORD will rescue me.

Oh how, my soul adores and exalts You. I acknowledge You as Jehovah Jireh, that great provider who knows and purifies my future as well as my past and present. You are well able to supply my needs and ease the weight of my problem.

You are Jehovah Nissi, the Lord my banner, who is powerful enough to overcome any problem that comes my way. I trust and depend on Your standard and will to always manifest in my life.

You are Jehovah Tisdqenu, the Lord my righteousness, who intervenes on my behalf and restore me to likeness and fellowship with You. I rejoice in Your righteousness to help me carry the weight of my problem every day.

Your Word declared that I can call on You and You will rescue me. Bless You now Abba Father for removing false teachings, misrepresentation of facts, injustices, and lack of concern for the needy and disfranchised of the poor are running rapidly across the land. Yet, Lord Jesus, the true son of God holds all things in the spirit of truth with the Father.

Cut through the heart of this argument to proclaim loudly that the weight of the problem by the witness of The Father, The Son, and The Holy Spirit shall operate according to divine timetable, calendar, and agenda of You. Because I am bought with a price, today, I submit my will, ways, and plans to You Heavenly Father.

4. IT IS NOT FAIR
Ephesians 3:17
[17] Then Christ will make his home in your hearts as you trust in him. Your roots will grow down into God's love and keep you strong.

So, Heavenly Father come now to hear and answer my prayer. There are times when life doesn't make sense, yet I will open my heart allowing You to it Your home. I choose to put my trust in You, Lord Jesus with all my heart and lean not on my own understanding. I desire and want to acknowledge You God in all my ways.

Give me, grant me, and show me everything I need to commit my thinking, understanding, exceptions, and brokenness to You, Father. My aim and desire are to serve You with a willing and faithful heart.

I repent of my perspective of only living life in a forward mode. I thank You for the clearest understanding of life's events when I see discouraging events, currently happening. Help me to see through Your rearview mirror to know just how You brought me through life challenges.

Yes, it's not fair that some things, the seen and unseen dangers, the plots, plans, diabolical sanction, injunctions, directive, mandate, and order that were devised, set-up concerning my life, children, grandchildren, family, and friends.

In the midst of it all, Heavenly father, there is something peaceful, relaxing, and soothing about Your rearview mirror perspective, in the Name of Christ Jesus.

It gives meaningful and accurate context to what I have experienced for Your glory.

5. REJOICED

Esther 8:17 - In every province and city, wherever the king's decree arrived, the Jews rejoiced and had a great celebration and declared a public festival and holiday. And many of the people of the land became Jews themselves, for they feared what the Jews might do to them.

Oh, how sweet, oh how precious, oh how wonderful, oh how blessed I am on this day to know the power of Your Holy Spirit, Heavenly Father. So, I cannot lose because my trust is placed in You.

Holy Spirit, have thy own way. Take the lead in my life today. I choose to rejoice in the province and city of our decree. As I turn to You, the veil of display, regrets, and conflicts are lifted exposing the cover-up, hidden truth, and concealed evidence are destroyed from my mind, heart, and spirit. Thus, I am well able to rejoice in You.

Every limitation in my life is simply an illusion causing my mind to create positively when it does not give power and light to false beliefs. Holy Spirit releases the flow of good in every situation today.

Manifest Yourself in my life as I am cutting the cards of false teaching, destructive habits, and limiting ideas and behaviors that no longer have a hold on me, my children, grandchildren, parents, family, and friends.

Today, I am free to be my best and most authentic self. I am empowered to interact with others in new ways. I make appropriate and constructive choices for my life. I rejoice and again I rejoice as I have the grace of God's incredible blessings over my day.

So, I will have a great celebration in You, Abba Father.

6. TODAY'S AGENDA

Isaiah 61:3 - And provide for those who grieve in Zion—to bestow on them a crown of beauty instead of ashes, the oil of joy instead of mourning, and a garment of praise instead of a spirit of despair. They will be called oaks of righteousness, a planting of the LORD for the display of his splendor.

Because You are Alpha and Omega, I worship You oh Lord. Thank You for this new morning where You looked beyond our faults to see every need in this glorious day. So great is thy faithfulness, morning, by morning, new mercies I see.

Today's agenda is not my own nor do I want it to be. Release me from myself so that I can stand in your agenda this day. Lord, have thy own way and will in my life today. Your plan and purpose are great. Release me from yesterday's tensions, stresses, hostiles, anxieties, self-blame and those specific situations that triggered these emotions. I place it all in Your hand.

Not only do I release my will and way to You, but I take refuge in You. I gladly rely on Your strength like no other to deliver and keep me. With today's agenda in You, I feel like going on Abba Father. Turn around my life in You today. Suddenly and completely change everything about me and give me a garland of praise. I take you at your Word allowing me to resist every foul fowl, every snare of confession, troublemaker, character assassin, plot and plan established for the demise of me, my children, grandchildren, parents, spouses, family and friends are null and void in the name of Christ Jesus.

Oh Lord, my God, how excellent is Your will and way. So, I choose to "wait on the Lord, to have my strength renewed mounting up on wings like eagles. I choose to run and not be weary. I choose to walk and not faint. Bless You, Heavenly Father, that today's agenda in You shall reign.

7. CHRIST'S PRESENCE

Psalm 143:7-8 - Answer me quickly, LORD; my spirit fails. Do not hide your face from me or I will be like those who go down to the pit. [8] Let the morning bring me word of your unfailing love, for I have put my trust in you. Show me the way I should go, for to you I entrust my life.

Maon, my Dwelling Places, who has promised to watch over me and keep me safe. I rest now in Your shadow, oh Almighty God. Satisfy me with a long life as I will sing Your praises today.

In Your presence, look beyond my faults to maintain and supply my needs. Because You love me, I will be still and know that You are God. Reveal who You are this day. Set the world right for Your glory. Do what is best in heaven just as I know You will on earth.

What more can I say but "thank You," Father for You and only You are the giver of all good gifts in my life. Thank You, for Jesus who died for my sins, transgression, and iniquities. Extend and keep Your grace and mercy new this day with Your divine presence.

In humble prayer, praise and worship you promised if I seek You, I will find You. Then allow Your love to fill and rule my soul in all those places of loss, conflict, misunderstanding, abuse, neglect, unhappiness, and financial lack. Fill my cup as I lift it up in Your presence, believing that you will forever quench my thirst within me. Bread of heaven, feed me until I want no more. I run for safety and security in Your presence today.

EIGHT - SYMBOLISM OF NEW BEGINNING IN ENJOYMENT

New beginning in enjoyment is **a sign of peace, and hope that can be sudden.** Yes, new things occur in your life as old things disappear. You can dwell in the process of taking pleasure in something with merriment and zeal. When you "Count It All Joy" with a new beginning in enjoyment, you rejoice in a variety of positive emotions and amusement.

1. HAPPY PEOPLE

Psalm 144:15 - Happy are the people whose god is the Lord.

Because You are the true source of happiness, strength, hope, and wisdom, I will always rest in these things. Even in times of prosperity or adversity, I am blessed, a happy person who is in the Lord's joy.

Your Word declares that "LIFE IS SHORT" as a breath and like a day passing shadow. Yet, You, oh God, give me strength for war and skill for each day's battle in You.

This day, I am happy to live for You Heavenly Father. I will not waste my time living by selecting an inferior purpose that has no lasting value in You. Continue to make my life worthwhile, purposeful, and meaningful morning, noon, and at night.

Remain my steadfast loving ally, strong fortress, tower of safety, and mighty deliver in all my ways. Stand constantly before me as a shield providing all I need to take refuge in You.

Make me happy when you bend down the heavens, Abba Father, and come see about me, Your child. Then stand tall to touch the mountains of despair so that your strong billow of smoke will blow. I want to be happy in You, oh Lord.

I rejoice in God's care all the day long!

2. A GLAD HEART

Psalm 16: 8-9 - Keep my eyes always on the LORD. With him at my right hand, I will not be shaken. [9] Therefore my heart is glad, and my tongue rejoices; my body also will rest secure,

You Abba Father are always at my right side; I will not be moved. How grateful I am that you will keep my eyes on You morning, noon, and at night. Yes, my glad heart is renewed in a sense of security, even though You do not exempt me from day-to-day life circumstances. I am cheerful, pleased and hopeful in all Your ways. Continue to show me how to move ahead confidently, trusting and believing in what is right in You, oh God.

With a glad heart, in You, Heavenly Father, pour out your loving kindness and tender mercies that will lead me, guide me and direct me along the path of honesty. Teach me every day to do Your will. Then calm me to enter Your gates with a sound spirit of praise to synchronize Your perfect will, agenda, and calendar with a fresh anointing that destroys every yoke in my life.

3. REJOICE

Philippians 4:4 - [4] Rejoice in the Lord always. I will say it again: Rejoice

Just to know You, Heavenly Father, that You are my only true source of happiness. I believe in You. No matter what You allow to come my way, my outer attitude will reflect what I know to be true in You.

I am grateful to rejoice that You, oh God did not leave me in my blinded state. Give me everything I need to use my "mind eye" to see what has never been seen, my mind ears" to hear what has not been heard, and "mind heart" to enter into all that You Abba Father has prepared, made and kept ready for me.

I am grateful to rejoice that You, oh God hold me in Your affectionate. Keep me obedient to Your Will and Ways recognizing all Your benefits bestowed unto me this day. I want my love for You Abba Father to do the talking.

4. A RESTORED LIFE

Psalm 126:5 - Those who sow with tears will reap with songs of joy.

With my hands lifted up in sacrifice, I bless You for giving me a long-life filled with joy, and happiness. You do great things. Not only do Your power release me from sin's captivity, but it leads me back to You.

Thank You, Holy Spirit, for searching me diligently, exploring and examining everything even the profound and bottomless things of God through Your divine counsel.

Those situations, behaviors, deeds, actions, and intentions within the hidden things that are beyond my scrutiny. Show me Your powerful glory; more of You and less of me is what I need. Your thoughts and will, provide me with all I need to discern those despairing in Your divine spirit.

5. STRENGTH FOR ME

Nehemiah 8:10 - The joy of the Lord is my strength.

This day I choose to enter into a celebration of life that honors You almighty God. You placed a good standard in my way, that filled me with joy divine. Because You are Alpha and Omega, the beginning and the end, a heart fixer, and a mind regulator. The joy of the Lord as my strength, I ask that You fill my plate with spiritual wisdom and forgive me of those negative behaviors that may wound the body of Christ. Purge my heart and mind with hyssop. Create in me the right spirit to glory You daily.

The joy of the Lord as my strength, Holy Spirit fill my plate and prepare a table for me in the presence of my enemies. Your joy has the strength and power to anoint my head with overflowing oil. Place a generous portion of love, peace, and meekness on my plate so that my heart rejoices in renewed strength and joy. Holy Spirit here is my coffee cup, pour an abundance of rich dark roasted grace upon my head. Fill my juice glass with gladness that will surpass my understanding that lean only to You, Abba Father. Then spread a nutritious slice of Holy toast with long-suffering, kindness, goodness, faithfulness, and gentleness allowing me to rest in You. I am ready to partake of Your eg-cellence of self-control in this joyful celebration with You.

6. FULL WITH JOY AND OVERFLOWING LOVE

John 15:11 - I have told you this so that my joy may be in you and that your joy may be complete.

Heavenly Father, I thank You for the mutual benefit between You and me that fills my life with everlasting joy. I lift-up holy hands. You are always gracious, powerful, majestic, excellent, perfect, and a strong tower.

I am grateful to dwell in Your overflowing love and joy to exercise and boost my prayer muscle to receive confidence in You. Joyously, I confess my sins, transgressions and iniquities. You know them Heavenly Father, as unhealthy, unpleasant and undesirable acts against the Body of Christ. I ask for changes to take place inside my heart, mind, and soul to gain positive prayer endorphins that set my captive spirit free.

Heighten my discernment to Your will and ways that equip me to live out the life You so generously ordained for me. Restore me with renewed prayer proteins to effect and enforce Your original plans and purpose over and against the plan and purposes of the enemy.

I bless and praise You Heavenly Father, for hearing and answering this prayer.

7. A FAITH PRAYER

James 5:13 - Is anyone among you in trouble? Let them pray. Is anyone happy? Let them sing songs of praise.

Heavenly Father. I thank You that when I am in trouble, I can call on You in prayer to seek Your face, asking for another chance that You look beyond my faults to see my need for your help and forgiveness. I am lost and out of control without You by my side.

Release me from my sins, transgressions, and iniquities to a new place in You. A new season of understanding that grants me all I need to remain in the press of a higher calling in You. What joy it is to rest in a new saving faith that will enlarge my territory and strengthen me to walk in the newness of life with restored divine purposes, honor, and boldness in You, Abba Father.

This day, I choose to rejoice because you know every plan and purpose ordained for me in this new season of faith.

With all that I am and all that I hope to become;

I will reach for you, Abba Father.

I will stretch my thoughts to receive from You, Heavenly Father.

I will incline my heart, soul, and spirit to walk in the newness of faith in You, Jehovah Jireh. It is my new season of faith.

*Thank You, Lord, for rearranging so many
things for Your glory. Amen.*

8. WHEN YOU HEAR THE CALL

John 10:27 - *My* sheep listen to my voice; I know them, and they follow me.

Because, I know you as Jehovah Shania, the one always with me. I am glad to dwell in Your secret place that is stable and fixed under the shadow of You the Almighty Refuge and fortress.

I lift up my head ready to confess my sins, transgression, and iniquities because I heard You call, "come to higher ground in me." You delivered me from the snare of the fowler and the deadly pestilence. You placed me under Your wings. There, I have learned to trust and depend on You as a faithful shield and buckler.

Thank You, Lord, for lifting my head to hear Your divine call.

I have hind feet to withstand the terror of the night, the arrows of evil plots by day, the slanderous tongues of the wicked that fly in the noon time.

Thank You, Lord, for lifting my head to hear Your divine call that will not follow another.

In Your grace and mercy, I have everything I need to let go of the deafening sounds of men's programs, plans, confusion, and opinions. Your voice is always clear causing my head to be lifted up in great expectations causing me to be:

- The head and not the tail.
- Above the noise of the crowd and not beneath them.
- Fearfully and wonderfully made to walk in the likeness of You.

Continue oh God, to take the lead in my life and release
me into Your marvelous hand. Restore peace and heal me
for Your name's sake.
Amen.

Delight in Joy

NINE - SYMBOLISM OF JUDGMENT IN HAPPINESS

Judgment in happiness is to **form an opinion or conclusion in an authoritative approach.** Well-being, flourishing emotional state characterized feelings of joy involving positive emotions. When you "Count It All Joy" with judgment in happiness, godly wisdom shines through you.

1. NOT A MESS, A TREASURE HUNT

Philippians 1:3 and 6 - I thank my God every time I remember you. **6** being confident of this, that he who began a good work in you will carry it on to completion until the day of Christ Jesus.

Because You are Elohim, the mighty creator, the beginning and end of all things, humbly I bow to adore and honor You in this new day. Bless You once more for the divine opportunity to begin again in You, a strong and fortified dwelling place looking beyond my faults of yesterday to meet my needs in this new day.

Because You, Heavenly Father is loaded with new grace and mercy for this day, my faith in You is tighten and secured as I press forward to release every negative thought, word, deed, or action from the assignments toward me, my children, grandchildren, spouse, siblings, other family members, friends, and associates in the name of Christ Jesus.

Gladly, my family and I stand firm in Your renewed strength as You forgave our sins, transgression, and iniquities. It is our desire to rest in renewed hope and courage to do what is necessary for this day.

There were times my family, friends and I made a mess of so many things yesterday. Yet, we are confident today of this one thing, that You loving Father God has begun a good work in us. Keep us in the treasure hunt for Your glory that nothing we said, did, or thought kept us from Your will and way for our lives.

Help my family, friends and myself to live and conduct ourselves in positive manners worthy of You, Lord Jesus, that are fully pleasing to You causing us to bear fruit in our good works. Put faith and love immeasurable in the hearts and minds of each one of us to walk by faith and not by sight. In the matchless name of Christ Jesus, we say Thank You. Amen

2. SAY THE WORD TO REAP A HARVEST

Matthew 12:31 - And so, I tell you, every kind of sin and slander can be forgiven, but blasphemy against the Spirit will not be forgiven.

> Lord God, Jehovah, the source of all faith. Humbly I pause in Your divine presence-basking in Your magnificent glory of a new day in You. You are my refuge, strength, a strong tower, and that steady bridge that guides me over troubled-waters. I believe and cry-out that Your faith is sufficient, pure, and true.
>
> I am grateful for my early rising in You this day which causes me to long for more and more of You in this day. I am grateful to seek Your immeasurable forgiveness,

grace, and mercy that is new every morning. Great is thy faithfulness. All I have need of this day, Your hand shall provide with compassion that never fails.

With gladness of salvation, I desire You oh god above all else on this spiritual journey. I focus my energy solely on You. I know how wise it is to begin my day with You to reap the harvest You ordained for my life today.

Mountains of sickness, depression, hatred, jealousy, envy, gossip, conflicts, wars, financial lack, dysfunction in family units, grief, and unemployment are ever present in the lives of Your people, yet You oh God, are well able to see Your children reap a harvest by Your word: "Be removed and be casted into the sea and do not doubt in your heart but believe that those things He said will be done, they will have been done." (Mark 11:23)

This day, I wait upon You, and the weight becomes lighter. I want to speak and do good things in alignment with Your word and the leading of Your Holy spirit. I speak life, hope, peace, joy, love, meekness, gentleness, preservice, and self-control over my life today. Thank You, Heavenly Father for a great harvest in You.

Amen

3. NATURAL EYES

2 Corinthians 5:7 - For we live by faith, not by sight.

This is the day, I know that my soul is anchored in Yahweh Tsebaoth the Lord of host, ruler over every power in the spiritual universe. Humble I bow to glorify your magnificent plans and purposes for this day. Continue oh Lord, to be my refuge, strong tower, renewed strength, and lover of my soul.

Because I live in faith and not sight, I seek to move from natural eyesight to spiritual eyesight. Give me everything I need to cry out to You as I face life's challenges in every area of my life. Hold my hand and give me all I need to release my fears and anxieties. I want to be armed with faith and confidence.

Release my natural eyesight to let go of all bitterness, resentments, envy, strife, and unkindness this day. My aim and desire are to draw every so closely to you. Yahweh Tsebaoth.

Guide my every step to uplift Your kingdom in the midst of struggles that lie ahead. Help me, restore me, and sustain me to be mindful that every situation or circumstance that comes into my life, is a battle that belongs to You.

Strengthen my faith with Your blessed assurance that cleanse me from all unrighteousness through Christ Jesus. Amen.

4. REST IN HIS HAND

Matthew 6:33 - But seek ye first the kingdom of God, and his righteousness; and all these things shall be added unto you.

Heavenly Father, I know that You have good thoughts, plans, peace, and blessed welfare that will give me a hope and a future in You. I choose to be still to completely rely on You by putting on the whole armor of God that will allow me to stand flatfooted against the wiles of my enemies.

I need the whole armor of You, Jehovah Nissi, the Lord my banner, that will allow me to withstand the evil, disappointments, and heartbreaking days to overcome my foes.

Raise up a standard over me and my family that will ready our minds for spiritual warfare. Give what we need to decree and declare;

yes Jehovah Nissi, those spiritual wickedness, principalities, and rulers of the darkness are too high for us to pull down in our strength. This day, we make the decision to seek You Jehovah Nissi. We want victories in You to be total and complete, casting out and destroying whatever stands in the way of Your plans, purpose, peace, and position for our lives.

Bless You Lord, that I can rest in Your hand.

5. IN WITH THE NEW

Isaiah 43:17 - Who drew out the chariots and horses, the army and reinforcements together, and they lay there, never to rise again, extinguished, snuffed out like a wick:

Good morning, El Shadday, the God almighty, one for whom nothing is impossible. Thank You for another glorious day that shall come in line with every plan and purpose ordained by You. Because I walk by faith and not by sight, in You I can command this day to sustain and bless me to fulfill every promise declared by You for me today.

Frustrations and failures have no place in this day for me as You took impossible successes and prosperity out of my timetable, calendar, or agenda. Old things have passed away as avenues of being the head and not the tail have become new in Your divine power and authority, El Shadday.

Because you are always available and with me, I have everything I need to press toward the mark of the high calling of You, El Shadday in Christ Jesus. I can delight and take pleasure in knowing anything or anyone assigned to undermine, frustrate, hinder, or devise a diabolical plan against me, my spouse, children, grandchildren parents, siblings, other family members, associates are friends are moved, cancelled rendered null and void from our sphere of influence now, in the name of Christ Jesus.

Continue El Shadday to release the joy of Your salvation into my life for Your name's sake.

6. RESCUE YOUR TIME

Ephesians 5:15-16 - Be very careful, then, how you live—not as unwise but as wise, ¹⁶ making the most of every opportunity, because the days are evil.

Heavenly Father, I bow to seek your face and hope in You on this glorious day You have granted me. Through spiritual eyes give me everything I need to see Your plan, purpose, will, and way today.

With renewed joy I praise Your holy name for being my Jehovah Jireh, the Lord a provider, who sees the matter beforehand to provide the need and rescue me in Your timing.

I thank You for all the blessings, forgiveness, faith, food and shelter, strength and wisdom, rest and work, and laughter and light that never come to an end in You.

Preserve and restore my time of refreshing in You. I want to pursue an everlasting relationship with You, Jehovah Jireh, to maintain grace to live in godly wisdom making the most of every opportunity presented by Your will for my life.

This day, I want to have my outward needs supplied according to Your all-sufficient power and energy. Help me to move inside Your will with an obedient spirit to follow your smallest command: "Walk by faith and not by sight."

Continue to be intentional to rescue me in You.

7. O GREAT MOUNTAIN

Zechariah 4:6-7 - So, he said to me, "This is the word of the LORD to Zerubbabel: 'Not by might nor by power, but by my Spirit,' says the LORD Almighty. ⁷ "What are you, mighty mountain? Before Zerubbabel you will become level ground. Then he will bring out the capstone to shouts of 'God bless it! God bless it!"

Heavenly Father, humble I bow believing, trusting, and depending on Your help to guide and direct me today. My aim is to get better acquainted with You, Jehovah Tsuri, the Lord my rock representing God's permanence, protection, and enduring faithfulness.

Since, I can always count on Your purposes and plans to remain firm in my life, I pray to rebuild my spiritual temple this day. Train my hands for war and my fingers for battle to withstand the obstacles of those great mountains that rear their ugly heads today. How grateful I am to declare You as reliable ground that I can stand on and in Your faithfulness. Jehovah Tsuri, thank You for hearing my voice and rescuing me when I cried to You. Continue to allow me to hear Your still small voice declaring, "my child, you succeed not by military might nor by your own strength, but by Your spirit, Jehovah Tsuri, the Lord my rock."

It is a blessing to know Jehovah Tsuri, that Your loving kindness is better, greater, stronger, and more desirable than life. So, I will bless You, Jehovah Tsuri and lift up holy hands to You.

In You, dear Father, every mountain is in Your control

8. ENTANGLEMENT GONE

Hebrews 12:1 - Therefore, since we are surrounded by such a great cloud of witnesses, let us throw off everything that hinders and the sin that so easily entangles. And let us run with perseverance the race marked out for us, "As God's official legislature and law enforcement agent, humbly I bow in the name of the resurrected Jesus Christ." It is You that I serve Jehovah Roi, the Lord my shepherd, who watches over me day and night. I bless and praise You for Your constant care and concern for my life.

There were days, weeks, months, and years that I wandered from your will and ways. Yet, Jehovah Roi, you gave nourishment to my body, mind, soul, and spirit to stay in the press in those dark times. Jehovah Roi, who kept me and allowed me to lie down in peace beside quiet waters for your name's sake.

Because You are my Shepherd, fear did not come near my dwelling place. I felt your present with me as Your rod and staff gave renewed comfort. You love, grace, and mercy. Jehovah Roi, didn't stop there; You prepared a banquet table before me in the presence of my adversaries. I was overwhelmed as You poured and anointed my head with everlasting oil causing my cup to overflow with goodness, love, self-control, meekness, and mercy. This day, Jehovah Roi, I am staying and dwelling in Your house forever.

This day, I kick off entanglements. Those negative actions, words, thoughts, and deeds that caused me to cheat on my relationship with You, Jehovah Roi.

Yes Lord, I am grateful!

9. NO WHINING

Luke 9:62 - Jesus replied, "No one who puts a hand to the plow and looks back is fit for service in the kingdom of God."

O magnify the Lord with me and let us exalt His name together. Jehovah Tsidkenu, the Lord my righteousness, this day, intervene on my behalf to restore me to your likeness and remain in fellowship with You.

Your way is perfect, tried, tested, and true to be a shield, buckler, and strong tower in my life. Your word declared that much work is necessary to let Your kingdom come and let Your will be done. Yes, Jehovah Tsidqenu, I am satisfied to receive my daily bread to deliver and keep me from all evil today.

In faith, I seek forgiveness of my sins, transgressions, and iniquities. I want to keep my hands fit for the journey ordained by You. With pure clean heart, let me dwell richly in all godly wisdom, with aims, desires, and resolve to meditate in You day and night.

Holy Spirit, Holy Spirit, lead me, guide me into all truth. Grant me clear understanding, discernment, and spiritual comprehension so that I am preserved for the snares of the evil one.

Jehovah Tsidkenu, my righteousness, grant me everything I need to reach beyond human reassurance to the limitless wisdom of the divine mind. Give direction to my spirit and illuminate my mind to release those situations and circumstances that are not of You so that I might focus on Your divine presence in every area of my life.

Thank You, Jehovah Tsidkenu, for life, hope, freedom, and an incredible reason to keep my hand to the gospel plow, for Your glory.

TEN- SYMBOLISM OF POSITIVITY IN EBULLIENCE

Positivity in ebullience is **the quality of being cheerful and full of energy in the practice of being optimistic in attitude.** When you "Count It All Joy" in positivity of ebullience, you are thinking in an optimistic way. Looking for solutions, expecting good results, and success worry free state of mind.

1. SHOUT IN TRIUMPH

Zechariah 9:9 - Rejoice greatly, O daughter of Zion! Shout in triumph, O daughter of Jerusalem! Behold, your king is coming to you; He is just and endowed with salvation, Humble, and mounted on a donkey, even on a colt, the foal of a donkey.

Oh Lord, my God, how excellent are Your ways. I seek renewed strength now in the quietness of Your Holy spirit. I want to dwell in your presence to worship, praise, honor, adore, and magnify Your holy name.

You are the omniscient one; the All-Knowing and Seeing, Great I Am. Fill me one more time with the light of You in this day. I seek to know Your generous love, oh God of renewed grace.

This day I can shout in triumph with huge mercy that will wipe out my disgraceful record. Then scrub away my guilt quietly, fearlessly, confidently, and boldly to draw me closer to You. I want to become whiter than snow.

Hear my weakness and aid my inabilities to produce good positive results that only you can do for me Holy spirit. Plead my cases unto the Heavenly Father for you alone know the unspeakable yearning and groanings that are too deep for me to utter without your assistance Holy Spirit.

In the quietness and renewed strength, Holy Spirit, intercede on my behalf according to the divine harmony and ways of You, oh God.

2. NEVERTHELESS

Luke 10:20 - Nevertheless, do not rejoice in this, that the spirits are subject to you, but rejoice that your names are recorded in heaven."

In-spite of what it might look like; I am delighted this day to rejoice in God's agenda and timetable. You are my refuge, high-tower, deliver, and way-maker, I choose to dwell in Your presence. I am grateful today that You are Jehovah Shalom, my peace, Jehovah Jireh, my provider, Jehovah Rapha, my healer, and Jehovah Tsuri, my rock of ages.

I seek Your forgiveness on this new day. Have mercy upon me, oh God according to Your loving kindness and tender mercies. Blot out my sins and wash me thoroughly, making me wholly pure. Purify me with hyssop to make me clean. My aim and desire are to be whiter than snow. Don't stop there oh, Lord, create once more a clean and renewed heart, that will preserve me with a steadfast spirit.

My mind is related now to be refreshed in your grace. Allow the blessings of you Oh God to make me rich and daily loaded with your benefits. Let this renewed spirit in You to bask in a fresh anointing that is crowned with your love and mercy. Grant all I need to see, feel, and know your glory with all good things.

Cause me to rejoice as you call forth those individuals and resources assigned to assist me in the fulfillment of your kingdom assignments during the correct seasons and timing for my life. Continue oh Lord, to take the lead in my life for your glory. Amen.

3. PART-TIMER OR FULL-TIMER

Romans 12:15 - Rejoice with those who rejoice, and weep with those who weep.

Lord, I thank You. Lord, I bless You for this day and redemption to set the captive free. Dismantle whatever agenda that may be perplexed against Your will and way for this wonderful day. You are worthy to be praised and honored for there is no one like You.

My aim this day is to remain in full-time status in the kingdom of God. Canceling anything or anyone assigned to undermine, frustrate, hinder or hurt me. I command that individual to move out of my sphere of influence and dismantle whatever agenda proposed for my demise, in the name of Christ Jesus.

This day, oh Lord, grant me full cooperation with Your plan and purpose that will set in motion a fresh excitement, a fresh mindset, a fresh zeal that is uncontaminated and uncompromised in the name of Christ Jesus.

I rejoice in my full-time kingdom profession and thank You Abba Father, that no matter what thoughts or worries are hammered out against your plan for my life, they are rendered null and void. I am a full-timer in the Kingdom of God. So, rejoice, again I say rejoice.

4. SO, I SAY!

1 Thessalonians 5:16 - Rejoice always;

Because You, Heavenly Father, has strengthened the hedges of protection around my life, I am well to rejoice. This day I declare that I am fearfully and wonderfully made in You.

Remind principalities, powers and familiar spirits that they have no right to touch my life in any way, for I am in a divine covenant with you, Abba Father. Continue to lead and guide me into all truth every second, minute and hour of this day. Cause me to listen, keenly listen to hear, just one word, to order my steps according to Your will, way, and original plans and purposes for my life, Abba Father. Teach me to know the power of your spoken word to reinforce and equip me for your glory:

- To be saved by grace.
- To be redeemed by the blood of Christ Jesus.
- To be a new creation in Christ Jesus.
- To stand as a part of the royal priesthood.
- To rejoice as a joint heir with Christ Jesus.
- To shine as justified by faith.

All I want on this day is to bless the wonderful name of Christ Jesus.

5. POWER, POWER, AND POWER

1 Samuel 2:1 - Then Hannah prayed and said, "My heart exults in the Lord; My horn is exalted in the Lord, my mouth speaks boldly against my enemies, Because I rejoice in Your salvation.

When I think of the goodness, authority, and excellence of the Heavenly Father, I can rejoice in His name. You God are the Almighty

One, a refuge, high-tower, a rock and fortress, a deliver, a shield, and the horn of my salvation.

Continue to be my stay and support bringing forth into us a large place delivering me because, You, oh Lord is pleased with me. Delight in all my ways. This day, I am grateful that you will reward me according to my righteousness, conscience, integrity, and sincerity in You, Oh Lord.

Look ever so closely Heavenly Father to see the cleanliness of my hands so that I may receive recompense in You. In Your power and goodness, Heavenly Father, I make the decision to take my eyes off hatred, gun violence, sicknesses and diseases, all those situations and circumstances that are negative behavior in this world.

Without doubt, I will put my trust in You. I pause to create glory and give it all to You. We want to cause You, Heavenly Father to lift-up off Your throne, stand up and take a seat among Your intercessors this day and you're moving forward with this "clarion call" to prayer from the correct position in the heavenlies.

Show me your glory. I want your glory. Less of me and more of You is what I need. Heavenly Father, I am depending on Your glory.

6. SACRIFICES OF PEACE

1 Samuel 11:15 - So, all the people went to Gilgal, and there they made Saul king before the Lord in Gilgal. There they also offered sacrifices of peace offerings before the Lord; and there Saul and all the men of Israel rejoiced greatly.

With all I am and all I hope to be, Heavenly Father graciously I humble myself before You. I seek Your grace, mercy, and unfailing forgiveness in all I have done and said against the will and ways of the body of Christ.

This day, I ask that you continue to have mercy upon me, O God according to Your steadfast determined love-loving kindness that blot out my sins, transgressions, and iniquities.

I ask that you hear my cries and wash me thoroughly to make me wholly pure in You. Then, purify me with hyssop to make me clean and with a glad heart. I want to hear joy and gladness causing my bones to rejoice in peace. Open your lips and mouth to show forth praises.

I am doing good pleasure unto You that You will be pleased with the sacrifices of righteousness of my broken and contrite spirits.

7. EXCEEDINGLY SIGHT

Matthew 2:10 - When they saw the star, they rejoiced exceedingly with great joy.

Because You know me, I ask that You take the lead in my life to empower me to make positive and significant deposits in the lives of others. Help me to maintain spiritual eyes that function with 20/20 vision to interpret and clearly see those suddenly, purposely, immediately movement in You, Heavenly Father. Yes, Lord, we want Your glory, more of You and less of me in this new day.

Today, I am extremely happy and pleased to see you and hear the good news of redemption one more time. I feel great joy and gladness to view and speak peace into my life, relationships, ministry, workplace, and business. Every path and avenue that are misaligned I command to come into divine alignment for You glory Heavenly Father.

This new spiritual vision will keep me from backsliding or looking back into old ways, old methodologies or strategies unless I am directed by You to do so, in the name of Christ Jesus. I can see clearly now Heavenly Father, since Your Word has become a lamp unto my feet and a light unto my path. I shall neither stumble nor will I fall.

When I look upon the star, I will persist until I succeed. Keep me in this renewed insight to see and believe all things are possible in Christ Jesus according to the will of the Father. Amen.

8. A SONG OF PRAISE

Luke 1:47 - And my spirit has rejoiced in God my Savior.

Oh God my help in ages past, my hope for years to come, my shelter from the stormy blast, and always my eternal joy. For You are God and there is none like You in the heavens and earth. With a humble heart, mind, and spirit I pause to bow in Your presence. I would like to tell You how much I love You, how much I adore You, and how much I bless Your Holy name.

You are that dependable rock of ages that clefted for me over and over again. So many times, I called and counted on Your power and might to pull out the sliding sand of adversities with the bondage of the past behind me and the roaring distant hope of Your promises before me.

With all that I am, hoped and thought to be, I have kept my trust in You. You are faithful and worthy to receive this song of praise. I worship You with joy, peace, love, grace, mercy, and freedom I have in You and You alone.

Continue to hear my humble cry for this day and give me all I need to push forward even when I cannot make sense of Your plan or purpose for my life. Pull me through, pull me through to release the jet lag that comes on this spiritual journey with You.

With clarity, confidence, and connection that You are always with me to allow the joy of my salvation to rise, shine and give You Lord all the glory. Amen.

9. REASSURANCE

Zephaniah 3:14 - Shout for joy, O daughter of Zion! Shout in triumph, O Israel! Rejoice and exult with all your heart, O daughter of Jerusalem! And may You shelter them, that those who love Your name may exult in You.

No weapon formed against me shall prosper and every tongue which rises against me in judgment shall be condemned. This day I am grateful to come out from under the tables of despair, conflict, disappointment, discouragement, sicknesses and diseases, negative thinking, soul ties, chains of captivities, deceptions set-up as decoys, plots and plans not of You Abba Father, I rest in Your divine blessed assurance.

It does not matter how many enemies from my past or presence rear their ugly heads, am equipped in You to shout victoriously that Your rod and staff surrounds me in comfort, goodness, and mercy.

I am right where I need to be as it is you Abba Father, that is leading and guiding me into all truth. Surely, you gave me dominion and power over the enemy, and nothing shall by any means hurt me. With reassurance, I declare that my spirit man is clad with armor of the Lord as my strength and the armor of His light as my guide. This day I walk in Your timing and conduct my life's affairs according to Your original plan and purpose for me.

10. EVOLVE

Luke 13:17-19 - [7] When he said this, all his opponents were humiliated, but the people were delighted with all the wonderful things he was doing. [18] Then Jesus asked, "What is the kingdom of God like? What shall I compare it to? [19] It is like a mustard seed, which a man took and planted in his garden. It grew and became a tree, and the birds perched in its branches."

Our Father, the magnificent One in heaven, hallowed, oh so holy is Your name. On this day, allow Your kingdom to come, allow Your will to be done on earth as it is in heaven. You are always the great and majestic provider. Thank You, for giving daily bread to take me from morning to night. Thank You for forgiving my debts letting me know how simple-easily it should be to forget my debtors, to remit and let go of debts against me by my debtors. Today, I am grateful to evolve in You.

Yes, the road is rough, the going gets tough, yet Your love, peace, joy, grace, and mercy inspire me to continue in your wonderful name. My aim and heart desire are to remain steadfast in faith right now-undisturbed by what is happening around me, my children, grandchildren, parents, spouse, family and friends.

Every second, minute, and hour of the day I am totally grateful that Your grace is an expression of Your loving-kindness always available to me. Your grace helps me to evolve when I am lacking the goods I need to survive for a time. I recall the many ways you cared for me in the past. Your grace helps me to evolve when I remember those precarious situations, failed relationships, unresolved conflicts that you worked out for my benefits.

Thank You, Abba Father, for Your grace-that unmerited
favor that I could never earn.

ELEVEN- SYMBOLISM OF FAITH IN ECSTASY:

Faith in ecstasy is **complete trust or confidence in someone or something having strong belief in God.** When you "Count It All Joy" you are faith in ecstasy. You experience an overwhelming feeling of great happiness and joyful excitement with an emotional religious frenzy involving an experience of mystic self-transcendence.

1. BE WITH ME!

2 Corinthians 13:14 - The grace of the Lord Jesus Christ and the love of God, and the fellowship of the Holy Spirit be with you all.

It is another day's journey, and I am glad about it. I have the opportunity once again to dwell in the presence of You, Oh God. Take the lead in this time of prayer, mediation, restoration, healing, deliverance, and forgiveness in You.

Set my heart to seek and search out Your will and way concerning all that You would have me do today. Open my mind to hear You speak inspirational thoughts so I might pursue You to possess a kingdom paradigm granting me new ways of thinking and living in You.

Help me to see those opened doors you have waiting for me loaded with a prophetic upgrade of my thought life to cancel the effect of negative, self-defeating thought processes and patterns putting them under my feet. Be with me to release everything prepared for me before the foundation of the world in its correct time and season.

Thank You, Abba Father, that I walk in
favor with God and man.

2. STRENGTH

Ephesians 3:14 - When I think of all this, I fall to my knees and pray to the Father,[a]

Abba Father, who art in heaven, hallowed and holy is your name. Lord, let Your will be done on earth as it is in heaven. Thank You for my daily bread. In your strength, I stand strong. Help me to walk in Your truth and not by my feelings, thoughts, agenda, or emotions. In your strength, I command my day to fully cooperate with Your plan and purpose for me. I want to embrace anything that comes my way as an opportunity to see You at work and as an opportunity to point others to You. In Your strength, let the anointing of the Holy Spirit flow uncontaminated and unhindered upon my life. In Your strength, give me all I need to repel every individual with a diabolical assignment in the name of Christ Jesus. In Your strength, saturate unconditional love deep into my soul and remind me that your mercy is new every morning.

I affirm that I am strengthened and spiritually energized with power through the Holy Spirit. I choose to   turn within to align myself with renewed strength and power with divine inspiration. You,

Abba Father knows the plans You have for me are to prosper me and not harm me, to give me a hope and a future.

I affirm that I am strengthened and granted insight to realize You want me to enjoy goodness in life and speak those things that are not into existence.

I affirm that I am strengthened to establish maturity, godly wisdom, authority, and supernatural abilities to bear witness to the splendor of Your kingdom on earth as it is in heaven.

3. INNER PEACE

Romans 8:5 - Those who are dominated by the sinful nature think about sinful things, but those who are controlled by the Holy Spirit think about things that please the Spirit.

Our Father in heaven, let your name remain holy. Bring about Your kingdom, manifest Your will here on earth as it is manifested in heaven. Give us this day's heart, no more, no less to fulfill Your plan and purposes. And forgive my debts, as I forgive those who owe me something. Lead me not into temptation but deliver me from evil. Let Your kingdom be and let it be powerful and glorious forever.

With inner peace, humbly I bow to adore You for who You are: the great I am, the beginning and the end, a refuge and a strong tower, the lover of my soul, a way-maker, a bridge over troubled water, the all-knowing, seeing, goodness and merciful One.

By Your inner peace, I confess my sins, transgressions, and iniquities now. Wash me thoroughly, Heavenly Father from my wickedness and guilt. Cleanse me from all unrighteousness. Shine Your light on the consciousness of my transgressions. I acknowledge my will and way to You.

Because of inner peace in You, I thank You for this new day, filled with joy, love, gladness, hope, grace, and mercy. Thank You for wisdom, strength, truth, and blessings in Your authority. I am thankful to command this day to function under Your divine protocol.

Clearly, I make my requests known with inner peace in You: take hold of the shield and buckler and stand up right now for my children, grandchildren, siblings, spouse, neighbor, community, church family and friends in the name of Christ Jesus. Draw out the spear and javelin to close up the way of those who pursue, harbor hatred, persecution toward those whose skin color is not like theirs, in the name of Christ Jesus. And clothe yourself now Jehovah Gibbor in Your garment of war to muster Your devices, gather Your weaponry, and spiritual ammunition from Your divine arsenal, in the name of Christ Jesus. Make bright Your arrows for all to see Your mighty hand.

4. PERSPECTIVE

Philippians 4:8 - And now, dear brothers and sisters, one final thing. Fix your thoughts on what is true, and honorable, and right, and pure, and lovely, and admirable. Think about things that are excellent and worthy of praise.

I choose to be happy today! Almighty Father, I might have thought in the past, that the scriptures meant that I was exempted from any kind of trouble as long as I trusted in You. Life's ups and downs had me to understand as one who lives in a fallen world with trouble all around me, that I am bound to face adversities, troubles, and crises. You know Almighty Father, that people have cheated, abused, hurtled, disillusioned one other over and over again. But the mighty waters of bitterness and hatred have not overcome me because in Your love and forgiveness, I have a refuge in You.

In renewed perspective, I choose to be happy and free to worship and praise You, Abba Father, in the beauty of holiness. I rest in Your unwavering power of infinite love.

Thank You Lord, that You have helped me to understand that my true self and authentic self are divinely powered by free will to guide how I speak today.

Thank You, that my actions are for the highest good of my brothers and sister today.

Thank You, Abba Father, that I am filled with Your love, filled with Your grace, and filled with Your wisdom today.

In renewed perspective, Holy Spirit, I need You every hour, minute, and second of this day to keep me in perfect peace. Bring forth reconciliation of brothers with brothers, sisters with sisters, mothers with daughters, fathers with sons, husbands with wives, and wholeness in the Body of Christ.

Renewed perspective magnets that are beauty instead of ashes and abund*ance* instead of humiliation to proclaim the favorable year of the Lord and shout-out the release of those in confinement or condemnation.

5. UNLIMITED

Psalm 16:9 - O wonder my heart is glad, and I rejoice. My body rests in safety.

Because You, Abba Father, show me the path of life by the Holy spirit, I celebrate in Your presence knowing there is fullness of joy. Today is a new day, filled with Your plans, agenda, and purpose making this day "unlimited" in You.

So, I humbly bow to set my intentions to meet this day with a sense of eagerness and great anticipation. By the Holy Spirit, I am counting on You to guide and direct me to draw uplifting and fulfilling experiences to me.

Stir up my gifts so that I can recapture the bliss, peace, and love that resides in my heart allowing it to flow through me for Your glory.

I want to feel new unlimited energy and elation overflowing from me with renewed sense of joy in every action, thought, word or deed encountered today.

Unlimitedness, allow me to dwell in Your ways because they are not like my ways. I want to surround my thinking with Your thoughts; for Your thoughts are higher than my thoughts. I want your calendar and time table to prevail, so I render my calendar and timetable void right now in the name of Christ Jesus.

Holding firmly and tightly to Your divine nature, that unlimited grace to release understanding of what is mine to do, and what is mine not to do in the kingdom of God.

Unlimited, all to You I surrender, I surrender all.

6. REST

Isaiah 25:11 - O Lord, I will honor and praise your name, for you are my God. You do such wonderful things! You planned them long ago, and now you have accomplished them.

It is times like this that reminds me, O Lord, I am not, nor my brothers and sisters are not in control of life and do not have all the answers. Yet, this helplessness brings me nearer to a state of panic, concern, fear, and uncertainties. But You remind me that You are always available to hear a call from your child. In the beauty of rest in You, I turn to You, call out to You, and put my trust in You.

Even when I find myself being independent and self-sufficient sometimes, I know to thank You Heavenly Father for a reminder that You are near, and I will never outlive my need for myself. I am glad to rest in You today.

Grant me the kind of faith that can turn my face forward to the tomorrow and the future transpiring this moment and time. Give me everything I need to keep my eyes on the best that is yet to come. Lord, my God, I rest completely in You. You are my strength like no other.

I am so glad when the tempest is raging and the billows are tossing high. I can rest in You. When I see the sky overshadowed with blackness and there is no shelter or help is nigh, I can rest in You. You let me know over and over again that You care that I perish not even when the moment is madly threatening, I can rest in You, Abba Father.

Get up, Christ Jesus, I need to rest in You!

7. JOY

Psalm 47:1-2 - Come, everyone! Clap your hands! Shout to God with joyful praise! ² For the LORD Most High is awesome. He is the great King of all the earth.

"As God's official legislator and law enforcement agent: I come in the name of the resurrected Christ Jesus. Whose I am and whom I serve." I say "good morning" Abba Father and thank You for the dawning of this new day in You!

With joy, I know that Your original plans and purposes for this day is to let Your kingdom come, Lord, and let Your will be done in heaven and on earth.

In Joy, I am so thankful that You gave me this day, loaded with my daily bread. I have Your forgiveness of my debts, allowing me to forgive my debtors, eliminating the wrong resentment to reside in my day.

Your joy is trustworthy and dependable, Abba Father because You know all things to keep me from temptation and to deliver me from evil. I am grateful for Yours is the kingdom of power and glory.

Keep me, fill me with hope that is loaded with joy and peace overflowing by the power of the Holy Spirit. Continue to give your hope of joy rising up in my soul again, again and again in You. When the enemy comes in like a flood, I have Your standard of joy to lift-up as my strength, Heavenly Father.

Thank You Lord, for "joy bells ringing in my heart, that sets the captive free.

Thank You Lord, for "joy bells ringing in my soul, that are firmly rooted, built-up, and established in Your faith.

Thank You Lord, for "joy bells ringing in my mind, that lets me know that I am being changed into the image of God, the Father.

Thank You Lord, for "joy bells ringing in my spirit, that says I am the elect of God, established by His grace and victorious through Christ Jesus.

Thank You Lord, for a new wave of joy flowing over everything in my path today.

8. PROSPERITY

Psalm 36:5 - Your unfailing love, O LORD, is as vast as the heavens; your faithfulness reaches beyond the clouds.

Abba Father, the creator of the universe, the awesome and mighty great I am, He, who restores my soul, the embodiment of wisdom with an infinite mind, humble I bow in Your presence to feast in Your abundance of loving kindness that I am unable to consume it all.

I confess my sins, transgression and iniquities against thee alone. Purge and wash me with hyssop, so that I become whiter than snow. Make me once again to hear Your joy and gladness. Surely, You can create in me a clean heart and renew a steadfast spirit within me.

Thank you for Your tender compassions that never fail and are granted to me, your child, new every morning. What more can I say, but great and beyond measure is Your faithfulness, morning by morning, new mercies I receive. Just keep my cup filled. Come and quench the thirst for You, that is inside me. Bread of heaven, I need and want You to feed me, fill my cup and make me whole.

Thank You for the prosperity of unexpected blessings that are coming my way in the name of Christ Jesus.

Thank You for prosperity that will do exceedingly abundantly above all I ask or think according to Your divine plan and purposes in the name of Christ Jesus.

Thank You for prosperity that let me know that I am special and the extraordinary fate that brings about new seasons of growth, in the name of Christ Jesus. Then, I shall feel and live in prosperity of You in every area of my life. Flow incredible blessings in my life today. Download immeasurable grace that is sufficient to guide and direct my day. Surround me in faith that is the substance of things hoped, and evidence of things not seen.

Prosperity, prosperity, prosperity, supernatural prosperity manifest yourself now. Show yourself might. Rain down your love, joy, peace, perseverance, kindness, goodness, faithfulness, gentleness, and self-control in my life now.

9. A PRAYER

Psalm 66:1-2 - Shout joyful praises to God, all the earth! ² Sing about the glory of his name. Tell the world how glorious he is.

Abba Father, who art in heaven, oh how hallowed, how holy is Your name. Thank You and bless You for granting me this marvelous day in You. I command this morning and day to flow in Your will that You have ordained for me this day. It is a new day to glorify and praise Your name. I am so glad to know that in You I can take authority over this day and every element of this day shall cooperate, stand in obedience to Your will and way with divine purposes and destinies.

I confess my sins, transgressions, and iniquities against thee and thee alone. Fill me with the light of day rendering me free to walk in the gladness of salvation another day. Oh, how grateful I am that You didn't allow me to yield to temptations and cancelled my seasons of frustrations, failures, disappointments, heartaches, misunderstandings, grievous sins, and unexpected illnesses and diseases to my body.

Because I am a citizen of God's kingdom, I walk in this season of success, renewed love relationships, overflowing in victories, renewed holiness and righteousness, and unending peace, love, and joy. I shout joyful praises to You, Heavenly Father!

I stand this day as the light of Your expressions and affirm the grace and mercy that surround and satisfy me today. Center me in Your divine presence with the blessed assurance that with You, nothing can knock me off balance.

In steadfast grace, believing, trusting, and depending on You, Holy Spirit, to guide and keep me aware of spiritual inspiration to remain in Your wondrous ways holding visions of joy, spreading from the hearts of every person in my home, neighborhood, city, state, country, and the world.

With shouts of joy, I thank You, Lord, and bless You Lord that I am calm and serene to rest, relax, and rejuvenate in the awareness of You.

10. COMPASSION

Micah 6:6 - What can we bring to the LORD? Should we bring him burnt offerings? Should we bow before God Most High with offerings of yearling calves?

Abba Father, who art in heaven. How hallowed and holy are Your name; Lord, let Your will be done in earth as it is in heaven. Thank You Lord, for my daily bread. I love, bless, glorify, and adore You for who You are; the all-knowing one, the all- forgiving one, and the all-righteous one. I pause to command and declare this is a new day in You. Because You created me as Your child, in Your image and likeness, I stand with hind feet over this day.

Thank You, Abba Father, that every element of this day shall cooperate with Your plan, purpose, and destiny in the name of Christ Jesus. In You, I have stability to stand firmly and progress on the dangerous heights of testing and trouble. Therefore, this season of frustration and failures are over in the name of Jesus. Because of who You are, Lord, I walk in a season of success, prosperity, good health, keen vision, renewed spirituality, and a fresh anointing of holiness.

Yes, I am delighted and excited to dwell in Your compassion that gives me a deeper and abiding love for all people. In the dawning of this new day, I extend my heart to widen my circle of compassion with everyone I encounter today.

With compassion for my children, grandchildren, family, and friends, Lord, look beyond our faults to see our needs. Lord, I thank You for renewed compassion, today.

With compassion, extend great faithfulness morning by morning to the schools and college campuses to receive new mercies. Lord, I bless You for renewed compassion and faithfulness, today.

With compassion, grant Your joy as strength that reaches in the doctor offices, emergency rooms, and hospitals. Lord, I lift up Your glorious name of Christ Jesus, today.

With compassion, pour-out Your power, love, peace, and kindness that fills my cup to overflow. Lord, I shout hallelujah You are my rock, my shield, and strong tower today.

Thank You, Abba Father for hearing and
answering this prayer.

11. PRAY CONTINUALLY

James 5:16 - Therefore, confess your sins to each other and pray for each other so that you may be healed. The prayer of a righteous person is powerful and effective.

I just can't give up now. I have come too far from where I started. Yes, Lord, I have not seen the manifestation of many answered prayers for those in my care, yet I know that You are with me. With Your mighty hand You are holding a rod and staff to comfort them and me in the wait.

Surely this day and everyday that You grant me is loaded with Your goodness and mercy that follows me to divine covering and protection to engulf me along the way. You know the plans you have for me. It is my responsibility to pray continually for those You have placed in my care, health, wealth, and well-being.

Give me the resolve to intercede and stand on my watchtower as you have ordained me. Favor me to work in partnership with You according to Your daily agenda and perform for an audience of one-the Lord Jesus Christ. Empower me to make positive and significant deposits in other people's lives. I pray for divine opportunities and occasions to help my family succeed. Maximize our potential and move boldly toward Your divine destinies ordained for our lives in the name of Christ Jesus. Amen.

TWELVE- SYMBOLISM OF GOD'S PURPOSE IN EUPHORIA:

God's purpose in **Euphoria** is the will of God or divine will in the concept of God's humanity plan. When you "Count It All Joy" in God's purpose and euphoria, there is a feeling of intense excitement with unrealistic physical and emotional well-being in God.

1. INNER PEACE:

Luke 10:5-6 - When you enter a house, first say, 'Peace to this house.' [6] If someone who promotes peace is there, your peace will rest on them; if not, it will return to you.

Gracious almighty Father, the all-sufficient, God. Humbly I come now to honor and praise Your Holy and righteous name. you are marvelous. A wonderful counselor, and perfect in all You do and speak.

Thank You for looking beyond my faults to see my needs every second, minute, and hour of this day. Fill me now with new grace and mercy to restore my inner peace in You. With all that I am and hope to be, I seek after Your peace that surpasses my understanding. My aim and desire are to walk in harmony with my brothers and sisters in the name of Christ Jesus.

Thank You Lord for new peace into my life relationships, ministry, workplace, and business opportunities. I rejoice in Your forgiveness of those thoughts, words, deeds, and actions that were not pleasing in Your sight. With renewed excitement, I bless you for creating in me a clean heart, renewed preserving and steadfast spirit within me. Heavenly Father, keep Your present with me. Lord, keep Your peace, inner peace, perfect peace residing in my spirit today.

In all that I am and hope to be, I am glad to call upon the power of peace to calm my emotions and remain centered in Your now faith. The enemy came in like a flood, but Your standard of peace restored my soul. Then, storm clouds rose, and strong winds did blow, yet in Your peace I held tight to Your standard of peace.

Pour out Your peace into my life, that shows me how to love right in You. In the name of Jesus, I prayed, Amen!

2. DIVINE ORDER

Mark 4:26 - 29 - He also said, "This is what the kingdom of God is like. A man scatters seed on the ground. [27] Night and day, whether he sleeps or gets up, the seed sprouts and grows, though he does not know how. [28] All by itself the soil produces grain—first the stalk, then the head, then the full kernel in the head. [29] As soon as the grain is ripe, he puts the sickle to it, because the harvest has come."

Jesus, Jesus, oh Jesus, no other name I know that brings comfort to my soul. So, I pause to tell You, thank You for this new and awesome day. Thank You loving and sovereign God that looked beyond my faults to see my needs.

So great is thy faithfulness-morning by morning new mercies I see. My failures, mistakes are a part of the "all things" that work together for my good. In today's divine order or agenda that is not my own, I release myself to You. Lord, have thine own way, will, plan and purpose for my life today.

In Your divine order, yesterday's stresses, hostiles, anxieties, feelings of neglect, self-blame and those specific things that triggered my emotions are in Your hands. I take complete refuge in You.

In Your divine order, I declare that You are my strength, strength like no other that reaches to me every second, minute, and hour of this blessed day.

In Your divine order, I am grateful for You turnabout in me today to decree and declare:

- In your divine order I take you at Your Word and reset every foul or foolish thought, word, or deeds that are not ordained in You for this day.
- In Your divine order, every snare of confusion, troublemaker, character assassin, plot, and plan established for my children, grandchildren, family, and me are cancelled now by Your mighty hand, in the name of Christ Jesus.
- In Your divine order, I take a stand that grants me everything I need to run through troops, leap over walls of destruction because You are my God. The God who grids me with strength and makes my way perfect. Oh, Lord, my god, I will not be moved until You move Satan aside in the name of Christ Jesus.

In this season of divine order, I surrender all unto You. Thank You, Abba Father for hearing and answering this prayer.

3. GRATITUDE

Acts 2:25-28 - [5] David said about him: "'I saw the Lord always before me. Because he is at my right hand, I will not be shaken. [26] Therefore

COUNT IT ALL JOY: A FAITH DIARY

my heart is glad, and my tongue rejoices; my body also will rest in hope, [27] because you will not abandon me to the realm of the dead, you will not let your holy one sees decay. [28] You have made known to me the paths of life; you will fill me with joy in your presence.

Because of who You are Lord; I humble bow to give You the honor and glory that is due unto Your name. You are alpha and omega, the beginning and the end. In You, oh Lord, I have learned that You are middle too. Loaded daily with great love and compassion that never fails.

This is a new day, and I am grateful that you look beyond my sins, transgression, and iniquities to grant new, huge mercy. You didn't stop there but You wiped out my bad record, scrubbed away my guilt, soaked out my negative thoughts in your laundry. You look at me through a different lens.

With a renewed sense of gratitude, I let go of my agendas, ways of doing things and exchange them with Your mindset guiding me to a purpose driven thinking.

With a renewed sense of gratitude, I receive a fresh anointing that destroys every yoke off my life and my children lives by the blood of Jesus Christ.

With a renewed sense of gratitude, I rest in Your lovingkindness that allows me to hear Your joy and stand firmly in Your trust.

With a renewed sense of gratitude, I remain in a plain path of righteousness to know which way I should walk in You.

I see Your glory leading and directing me on this day. Keep me ever mindful that I am Yours, Heavenly Father. I was bought with a price and thine will be done in my life.

4. HOPE AND FAITH

Hebrews 11:1-3 -_Now faith is confidence in what we hope for and assurance about what we do not see. [2] This is what the ancients were commended for. [3] By faith we understand that the universe was formed at God's command, so that what is seen was not made out of what was visible.

Good morning, Abba Father! Oh, how great is Your faithfulness. Morning by morning, new deliberate mercies I see from You. It does not run out, does not dry up, and does not spring a leak. Today and every day, Abba Father, I am sticking with You. You looked beyond all my yesterdays' faults to give me this day to dwell in Your presence because You are available and ready to hear Your children pray.

My hope and faith are companions that bring my "If I self" with all my flaws, frustrations, unresolved thinking, brokenness, and misconceptions of what is happening in my home, family, on the job, in the school house, and community that disturb our spiritual equilibrium on life's journey.

Heavenly Father, I am in need of Your balance that resides in "now faith that is the assurance of things hoped and the conviction for things not seen."

Your balance of hope and faith allows me to peek through the window of hope to glimpse the good that is yet to come into my life for Your glory.

Your balance of hope and faith causes me to replenish, let go of the "If I Self" and put on the armor of hope and faith in You, Heavenly Father.

Kindle my zeal, imagination, and love to realize that the good that I am hoping for is already mine in You, Christ Jesus. Every second, minute, and hour of my day is already planned out in You.

Thank You, Lord, for hope and faith to order my day.

5. WONDER!

Matthew 18:2-4 - ² He called a little child to him, and placed the child among them. ³ And he said: "Truly I tell you, unless you change and become like little children, you will never enter the kingdom of heaven. ⁴ Therefore, whoever takes the lowly position of this child is the greatest in the kingdom of heaven.

In Your perspective, Heavenly Father, I humbly bow in accordance with Your will for this day. I glorify Your wonderful and awesome name that is above every name.

Because You are Abba Father, the great I am, an excellent deliverer, and a way maker. I exalt You:

As Jehovah Shalom-my peace that surpasses all understanding gives me "wholeness," "completeness," "perfection," "safety, and "wellness in my inner calmness.

As Jehovah Tsidkenu-my righteousness in Christ Jesus placing me in the right relationship with God.

As Jehovah Jireh-my provider that sees the future as well as the past. You are well able to anticipate my needs.

As Jehovah Rophe - my healer, restore. Continue to search my heart and show me what it contains to bring divine forgiveness and healing.

As Jehovah Tsuri-my rock loaded daily with permanence, protection, and enduring faithfulness. My heart, mind, and soul are thankful that I can always count on You, Jehovah Tsuri.

You are a "wonder." I am nothing without You.

6. CELEBRATE

Proverbs 15:12-13 - ² Mockers resent correction, so they avoid the wise. ¹³ A happy heart makes the face cheerful, but heartache crushes the spirit.

Heavenly Father, the creator of this universe, the great I am. You are holy, hallowed, majestic, and excellent in all Your ways.

So, forgive my debts as I forgive those who trespass against me. Keep me, that I am not led into temptations. Forgive me of any thoughts, words, deeds, actions, or emotions that wounded the Body of Christ.

I am thankful to have this opportunity to celebrate this new day in You. I realize that nothing I did or said yesterday afforded me this divine privilege to be here this day.

Your great mercies, unfailing love, and enormous compassion has blotted out the stains of sins, washed me clean from my transgressions and iniquities.

Thank You, Lord for a clean heart, and renewed spirit within me.

Please don't take, banish, or remove Your presence from me. I need and want Your continuous peace to operate in my life.

Yes, I celebrate life today. Filled with love, joy, peace, hope, and glory knowing that without a shadow of doubt, that You, God are with me. You serve me a six-course dinner right in front of my enemies. Look how you revive my drooping head, causing my cup brim to fill with blessings.

I celebrate life today. Your beauty and love have chased after me causing my belief system to swell and not perish. I have eternal life in You. Live in me and take control of my life with the enormous power of Christ Jesus.

Thank You, Lord, that I shine with a special radiance that brings happiness and well-being into my life.

7. RENEWED PURPOSE

2 Chronicles 7:14-15 - If my people, who are called by my name, will humble themselves and pray and seek my face and turn from their wicked ways, then I will hear from heaven, and I will forgive their sin and will heal their land. [15] Now my eyes will be open and my ears attentive to the prayers offered in this place.

My Father in heaven, let Your name remain holy. Bring about Your kingdom-manifest Your will here on earth as it is in heaven. Give me today's heart no more-no less to fulfill Your plans and purposes. And forgive me debts, as I forgive those who owe me debts. Lead me not into temptation but deliver me from evil. Lord, let Your kingdom be and let it be powerful and glorious forever.

Because You brought me through the trails, the obstacles, the test, the disappointments, the death of loved ones, sicknesses and diseases, misunderstanding in my family, marriage conflicts, broken relationships, financial lack, unemployment, loss of personal possessions, cluttered of thoughts, and no mutation, I look forward to Your renewed purposes in my life.

Thank You for grace that gave me another chance-a day-a week-a month- and another year to get it right and lift up holy hands unto You, Oh Lord, my God.

In this season of renewed purpose, govern my thoughts with only those things that are true, noble, reputable, authentic, compelling, and gracious that are the best of You, Abba Father.

In this season of renewed purpose. Allow this prayer to take control over the airways, social media, galaxies, atmosphere, regions, domain according to You word in Psalm 103:20 "Angels now excel in strength to marshal and protect my personage: children, grandchildren, neighborhoods that will cause the evil devices of the evil one to surrender unto Your will and way, now, in the name of Christ Jesus.

In this season of renewed purpose, I stand in the gap as an intercessor, seeking Your face, asking You to contend with those things that are not pleasing in Your sight. Fight against those that fight against what is right to heal the land. Heavenly Father, I am asking that You heal the land now for Your glory. Amen!

8. MESSAGE OF WISDOM

1 Corinthians 2: 9-16 - However, as it is written: "What no eye has seen, what no ear has heard, and what no human mind has conceived"[a] the things God has prepared for those who love him— [10] these are the things God has revealed to us by his Spirit. The Spirit searches all things, even the deep things of God. [11] For who knows a person's thoughts except their own spirit within them? In the same way no one knows the thoughts of God except the Spirit of God. [12] What we have received is not the spirit of the world, but the Spirit who is from God, so that we may understand what God has freely given us. [13] This is what we speak, not in words taught us by human wisdom but in words taught by the Spirit, explaining spiritual realities with Spirit-taught words.[b] [14] The person without the Spirit does not accept the things that come from the Spirit of God but considers them foolishness, and cannot understand them because they are discerned only through the Spirit. [15] The person with the Spirit makes judgments about all things, but such a person is not subject to merely human judgments, [16] for, "Who has known the mind of the Lord so as to instruct him?"[c] But we have the mind of Christ.

In a spirit of humility, I pause now to adore Your excellent power and majestic way, Heavenly Father. I receive your immeasurable grace and mercy that is available to me, new every morning. Just let me rest in Your unfailing love and compassion today.

Forgive my debts, sins, transgressions, and inequities. Wash me of all my guilt and shame. Make me whiter than snow to create a clean heart and renewed right spirit.

Your message of wisdom lets me know that I am nothing without You. I need You to dwell and stay put in every area of my life.

Let Your message of wisdom take authority over this day to declare that every element of this day shall cooperate with Your divine purpose and destiny. Continue to say some big things to me and my children by Your divine Spirit to inspire deeds, dreams, and declarations put out into the open before us.

Instill Your message of wisdom to push me beyond my natural abilities and into Your arms of supernatural abilities. Cause my eyes to see what has not been seen, my ears to hear what has not been heard, and my heart to receive what no man has ever received for Your glory.

Thank You, Abba Father for a message of wisdom, today.
Amen!

9. RELAX

Psalm 23:1 - The Lord is my shepherd, I lack nothing.

I am thine oh, Lord, so draw me nearer in Your perfect will and way. So, I lift up holy hands asking You to fill my cup with Your presence. Give me everything I need to recognize and bless Your perfect design for my life today. Establish everything I need to harmonize myself with Your inner unfoldment to visit and let go of the mind clutter. My desire is to rest and relax in You.

Yes, the conflicts of life, disappointments of self, negative outcomes, and other impatience of waiting on unanswered prayers has caused my soul to detach itself from Your truth. I need Your spiritual intuition and feeling of peace to saturate my deepest thoughts in You.

I am glad that You are my shepherd. Continue to feed me, guide me, hide me, restore me, shield me from the scourge of the enemy. For in Your presence nothing is lacking, nothing is missing, and nothing is falling apart.

So, I take this time to relax and lie down in fresh tender green pastures-by still and restful waters. Relaxing and waiting for You to lead me in the paths of righteousness and uprightness for Your name's sake. Then synchronize my path with clear and straight directions so that I will not trip or fall because You are holding my hands.

Thank You, Lord as I relax in You:

- My strength is renewed.
- My personal and spiritual growth are restored.
- My work becomes my worship.
- My potential is maximized to the more.
- My ministry is assigned only relationships that enhance my life for this season.
- My days are best and blessed.
- My family, home, finances, and job function smoothly and efficiently in the name of Christ Jesus.
- I delight myself by sitting at a prepared table just for me in the presence of every naysayer, discourager, those envious and jealous folks that are onlookers to my life.
- Thank You Lord, that my head is anointed with oil. My cup runs over to the brim. Amen!

10. YOU ARE GETTING WARMER

2 Timothy 3:16-17 - [6] All Scripture is God-breathed and is useful for teaching, rebuking, correcting and training in righteousness, [17] so that the servant of God[a] may be thoroughly equipped for every good work.

This morning is a glorious, glorious day in You. So, I shout hallelujah and bless Your holy name Abba Father. Continue to help me to keep getting warmer as I study Your inspired Word Heavenly Father. It is trustworthy. It is a lamp unto my feet. It is a divine standard for testing everything else that claims to be true.

Allow us to apply Your work as a safeguard against false teaching and a great source of guidance for how You asked us that we walk by faith and not by sight in You. This day is my desire to read Your word regularly to discover and keep God's truth in my heart, mind, soul, and spirit. I want to develop a plan to read Your Word every day.

In my zeal for the truth of Your Word to keep me getting warmer, bring inspirational thoughts, readings, songs, to equip me to do good. I want to study Your word to increase my knowledge of You and to do Christ's work in this world for Your glory Heavenly Father. Strengthen my faith and lead me in Your divine path for Your name's sake. Amen.

11. THE MIND OF CHRIST

2 Corinthians 2:16 - For, "Who has known the mind of the Lord so as to instruct him?" [But we have the mind of Christ.

Holy Spirit, Holy Spirit, I bow to learn how to fill my mind with good, godly great thoughts for this day. My aim and desire are to "fix my thoughts on what is true, honorable, right, pure, lovely, and admirable." I know that such thought is excellent and worthy of praise.

Transform my mind and thoughts to have kingdom power to elevate my life to kingdom worship and praise. Give me everything I need to become extremely "vigilant" about my mind this day. Whatever I hear, give me the resolve to not allow it to affect what I think or believe if it isn't of Your truth. Grant me renewed grace to heed what I might say to others as well as what others might say to me.

Help me to become adequate for the task of representing Christ in every word, thought, action, and deed I perform this day. I know Heavenly Father that this adequacy must come from You. You commissioned me in Matthew 28: 18-20 to go in the Holy Spirit to speak with Christ's power and authority.

I want to have life-affirming thoughts of success and prosperity filling my ears with words that will produce kingdom thinking for my life and all those in my care according to the Holy Spirit. Thank You, Holy Spirit for this kingdom revelation for this day. I want to grasp, hold ever so tightly the will of the Lord for my life. Amen.

12. MAJESTIC AND HOLY

Ecclesiastes 12:13 - [3] Now all has been heard; here is the conclusion of the matter: Fear God and keep his commandments, for this is the duty of all mankind.

Loving and kind Father god, I pause in Your divine presence to stand clearly in Your Word. "With God all things are possible." Your beloved Son, Jesus Christ, showed me the way when He prayed at Gethsemane and surrendered His will, ways, and agenda to Your perfect plan. In Christ, I pause in Your awesomeness, Heavenly Father.

Through this hope in You, I pray that You allow me to hear Your loving kindness on this day, for it is in You do I put all my trust. I ask once again that You would cause me, oh God, to know the way in which I should walk, talk, and have my being. I lift-up my soul unto You.

Teach me, guide me, and direct me to do Your will with questions. Your Holy Spirit is God; continue to lead me in the land of uprightness. I want to feel the flame of the same type of hope You gave Christ Jesus by Your majestic power in my heart this day.

Heavenly Father, of the impossible, grant me by Your grace an ample supply of hope for this day. Strengthen me now and grant me that hope for impossible situations to become possible according to Your grace that is sufficient for this day. Restore, deliver, and set the captive free to remain faithful in the press toward the mark of the high calling of God in Christ Jesus.

This glorious day by a fresh anointing, "every yoke is broken off my life and is destroyed; every burden is lifted. Thank you, Majestic Heavenly Father, for allowing me to know that Your yoke is easy, and burden is light.
Amen!

RESOURCES:

1. More than Conquerors by Christian Art Publishers
2. Praying the Names of God-A Daily Guide by Ann Spangler
3. Commanding Your Morning, by Dr, Cindy Trimm
4. The Life Application Bible
5. Daily Word by Unity Publication Prayer Ministry
6. The Message Bible
7. The Amplified Bible

References:
Source: https://bible.knowing-jesus.com/words/Jubilation
Source: https://bible.knowing-jesus.com/topics/Rejoicing

ABOUT THE AUTHOR

Janet Williams-Johnson-MEd, is a dedicated and compassionate Early Childhood Educator, an Elementary School Administrator, and Academic Engagement and Curricula Specialist, who loves interacting with various elementary school communities' stakeholders. Her motivation strategies are designed to enhance and strengthen relevant intervention learning initiatives using individualized and cooperative curricula. Janet's years of experience developing instructional plans across various grade levels are instrumental in her writing this devotional trilogy.

Janet hopes this book will allow you to dive deeper into the biblical study outlined from her many years of using the Word of God to write prayers.

www.ingramcontent.com/pod-product-compliance
Lightning Source LLC
Chambersburg PA
CBHW051541120626
46551CB00013B/1322